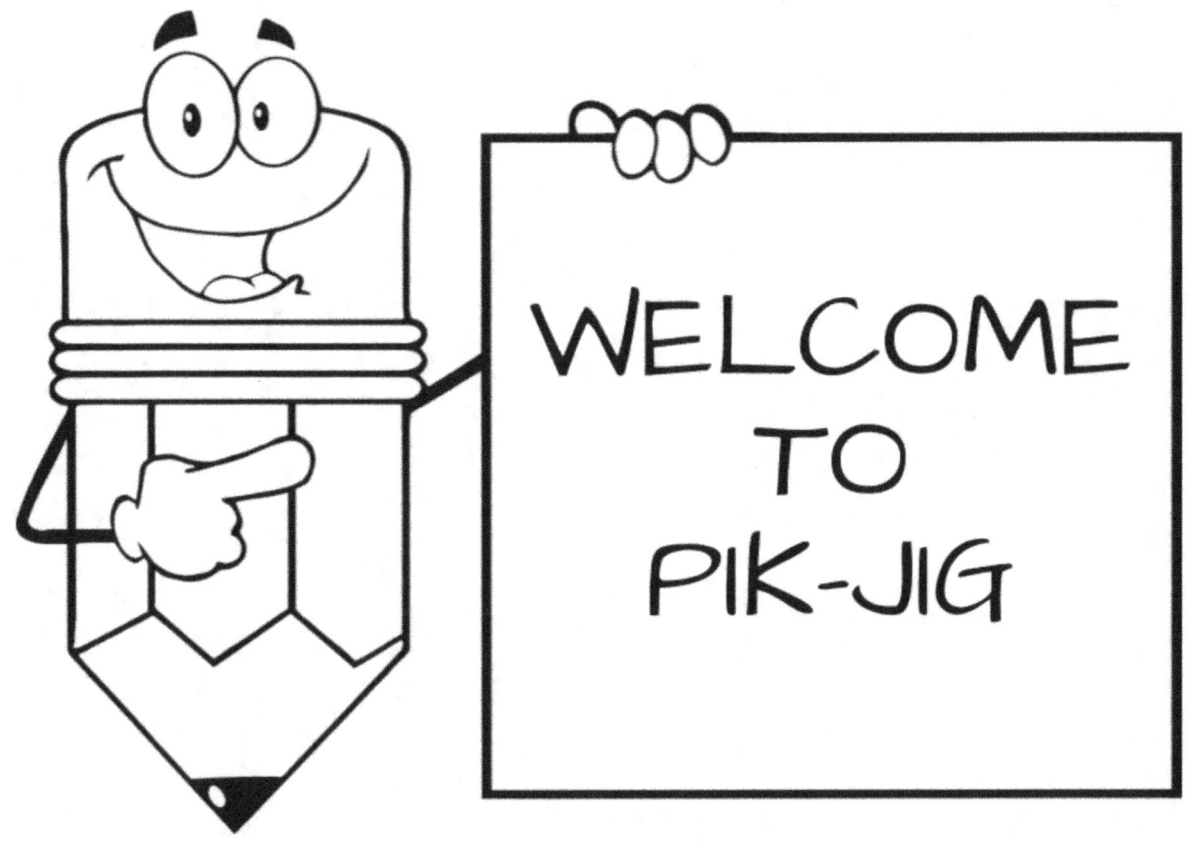

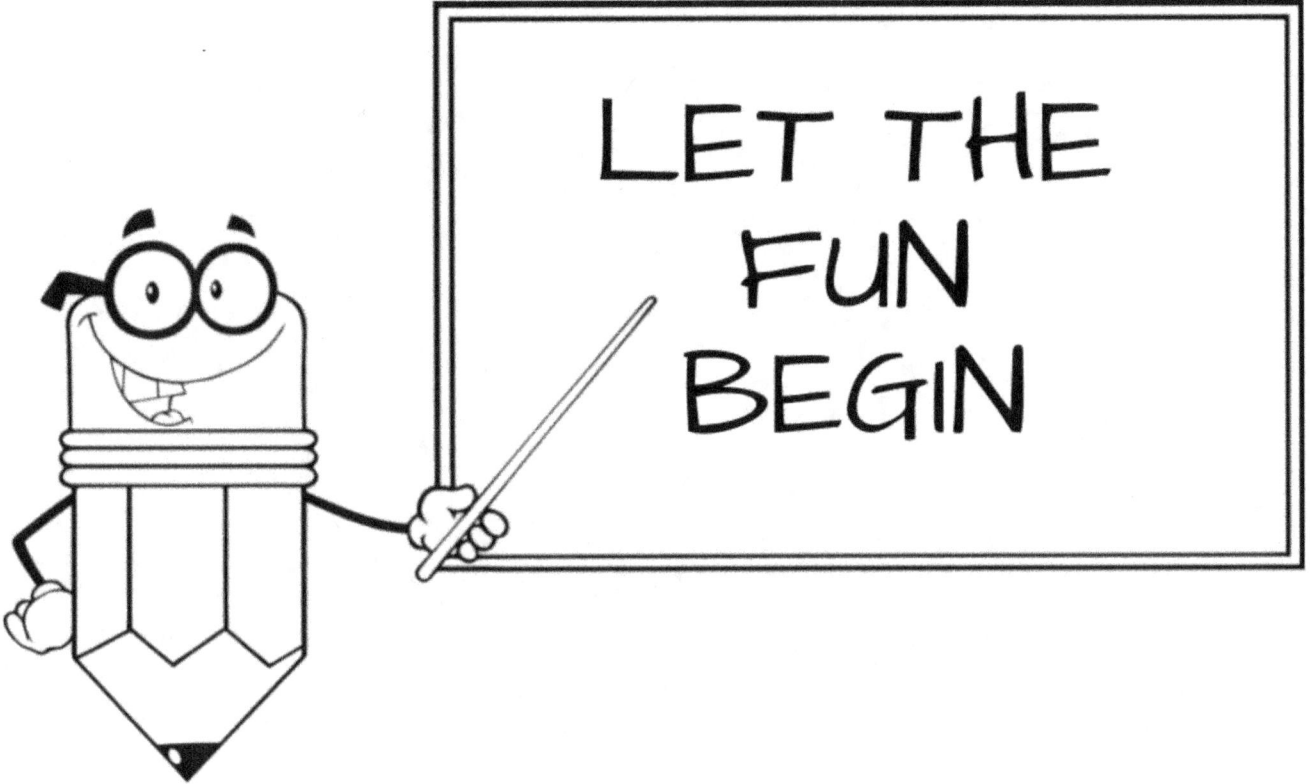

INSTRUCTIONS

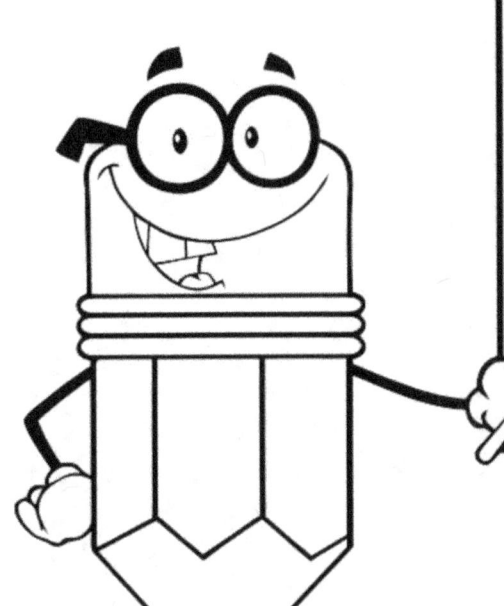

STEP ONE
PICK A SQUARE

STEP TWO
FIND THE SQUARE ON THE GRID BY
MATCHING THE COORDINATES

STEP THREE
DRAW WHAT YOU SEE AND WATCH
THE MAGIC UNFOLD

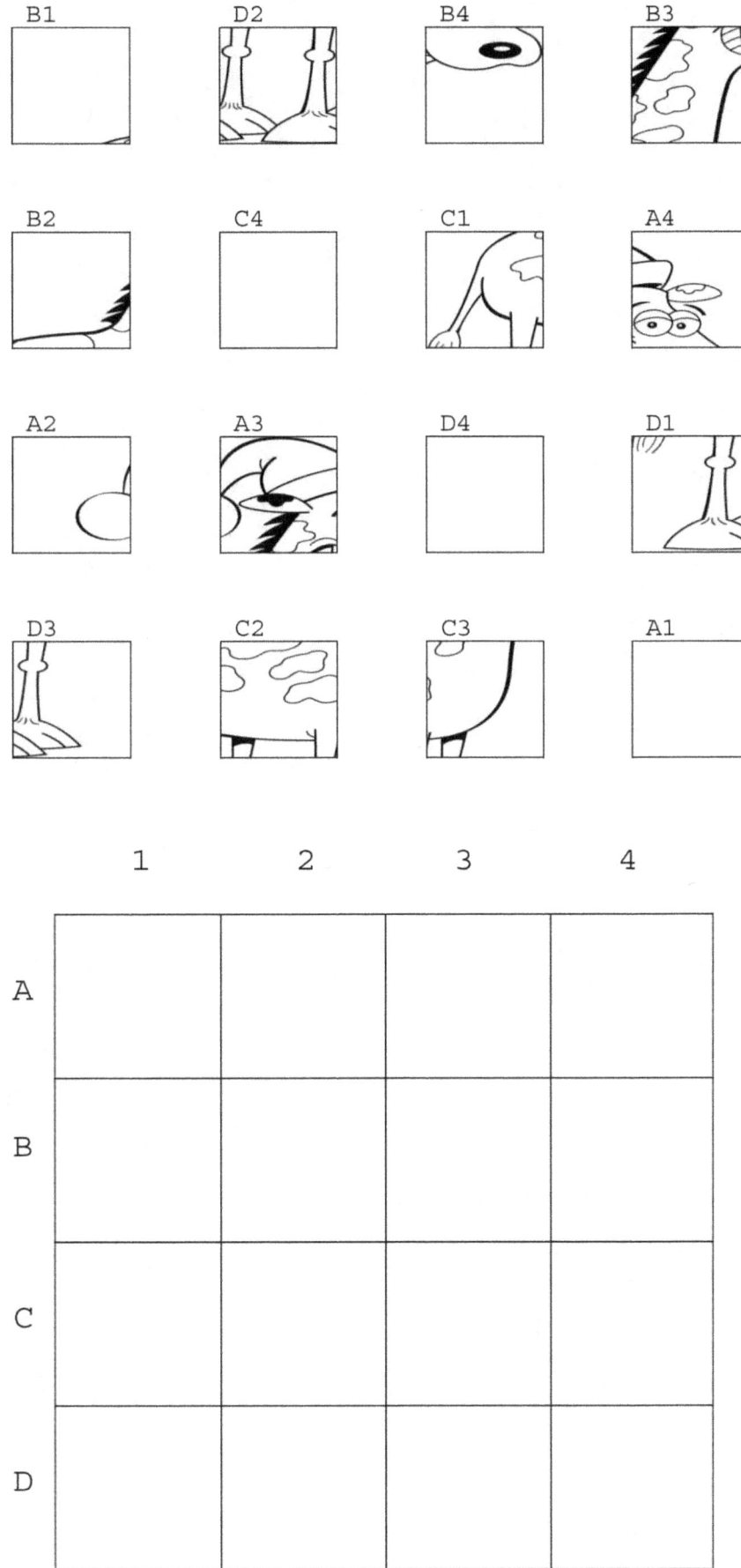

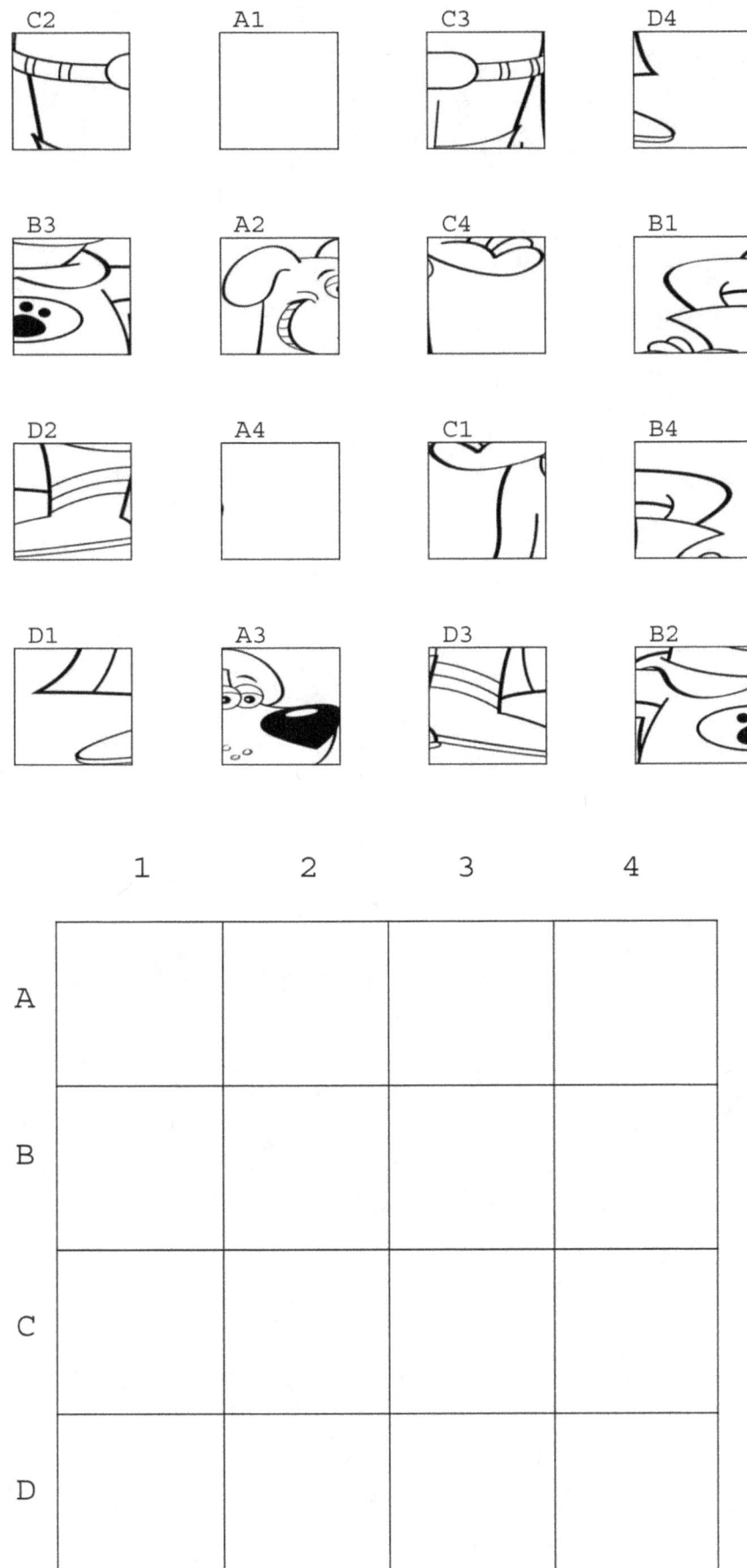

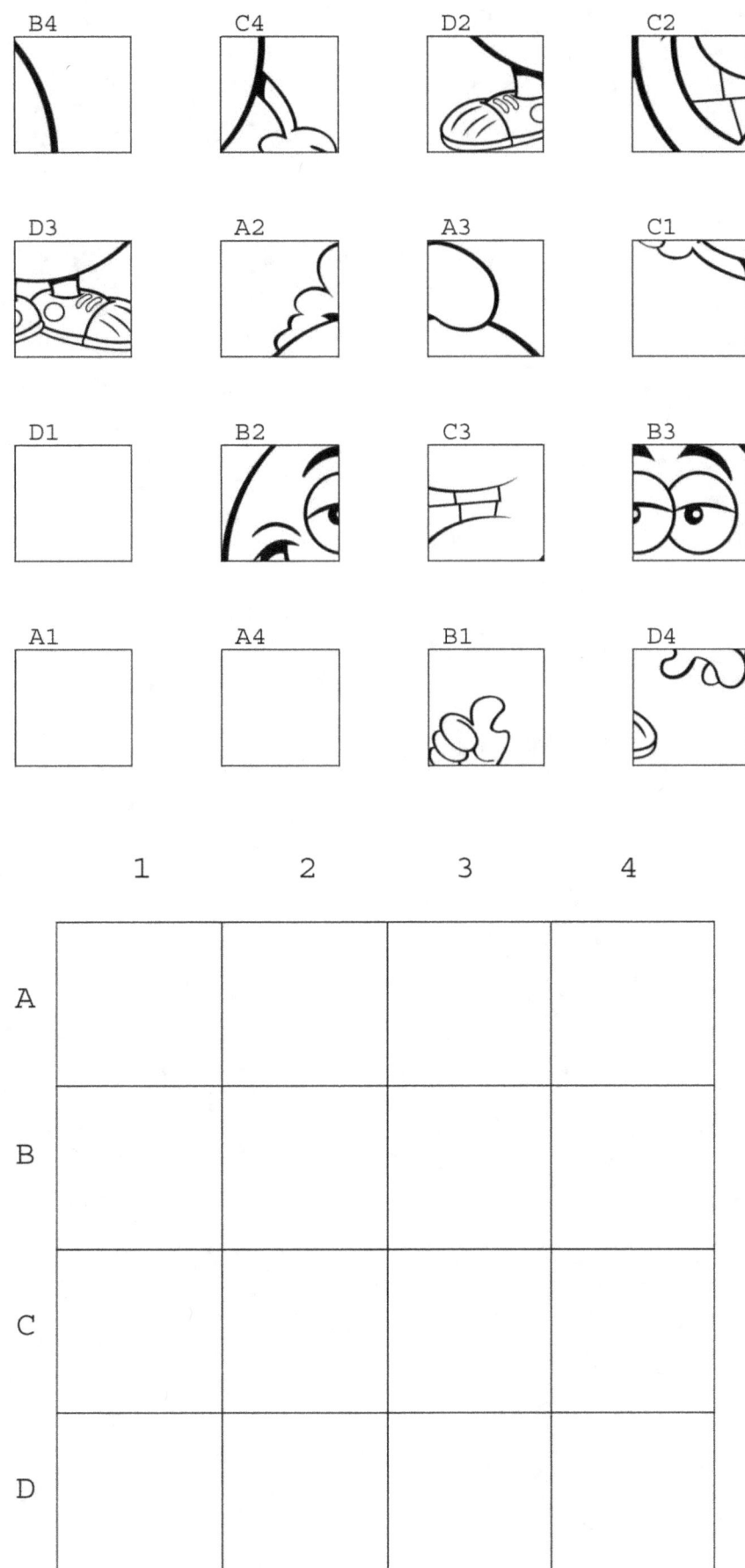

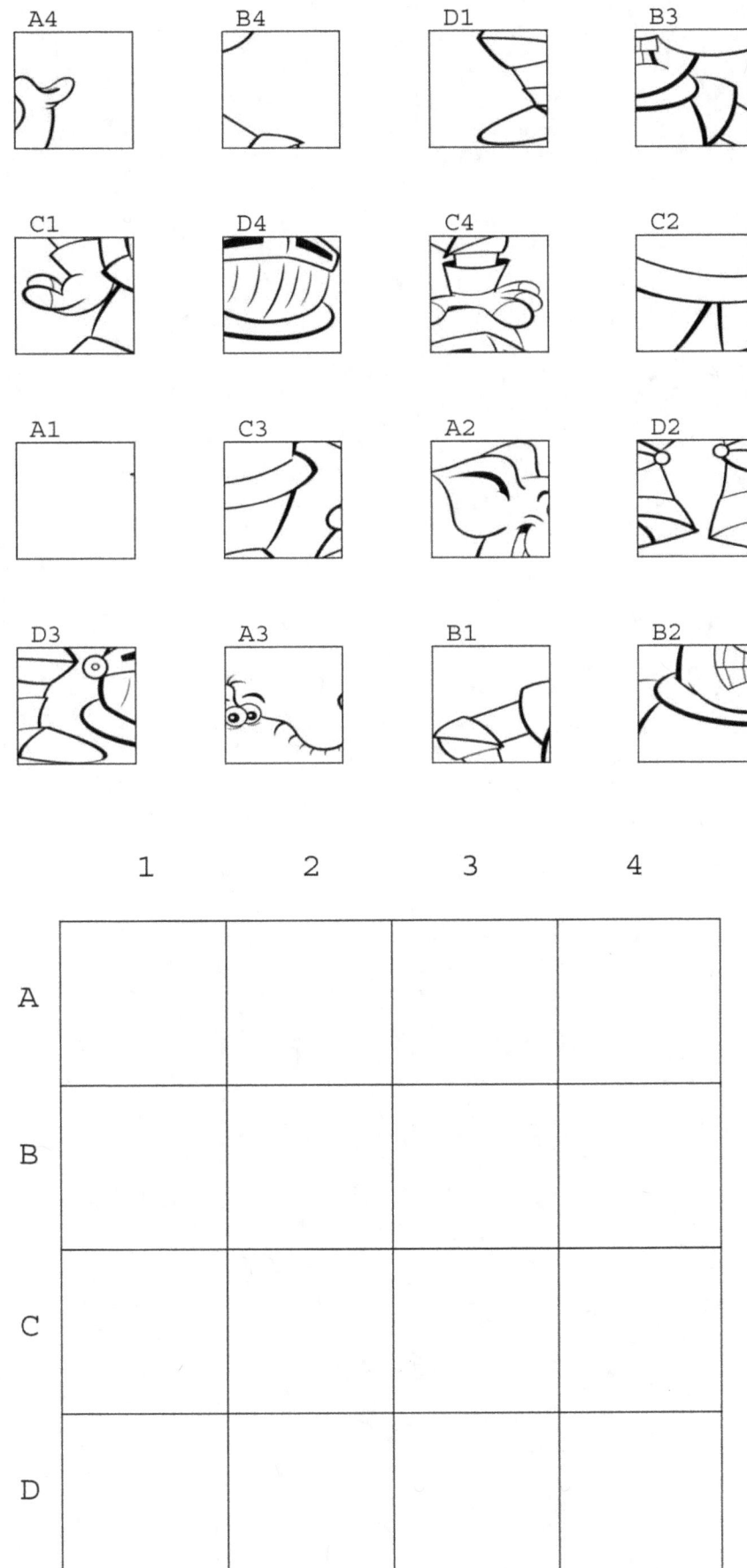

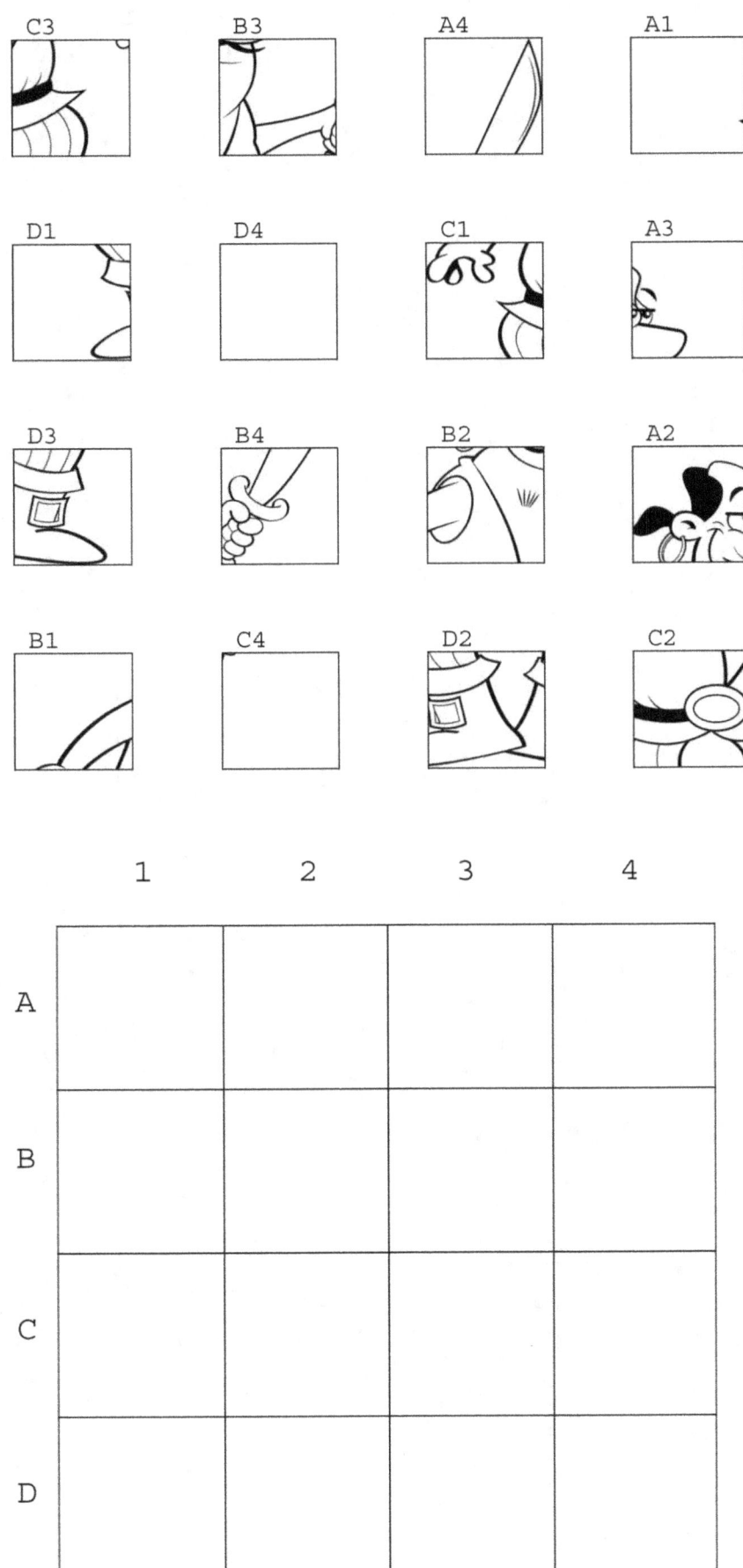

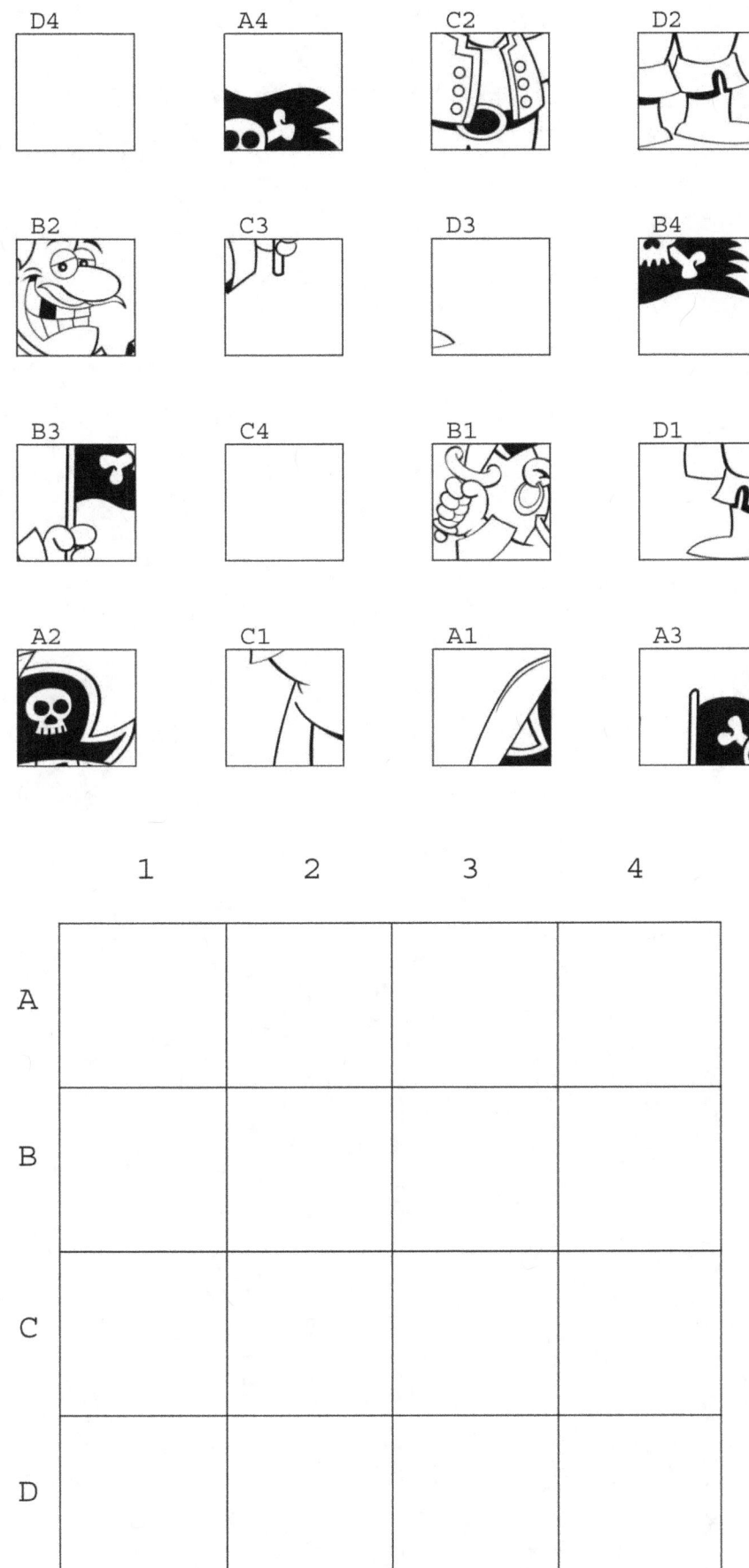

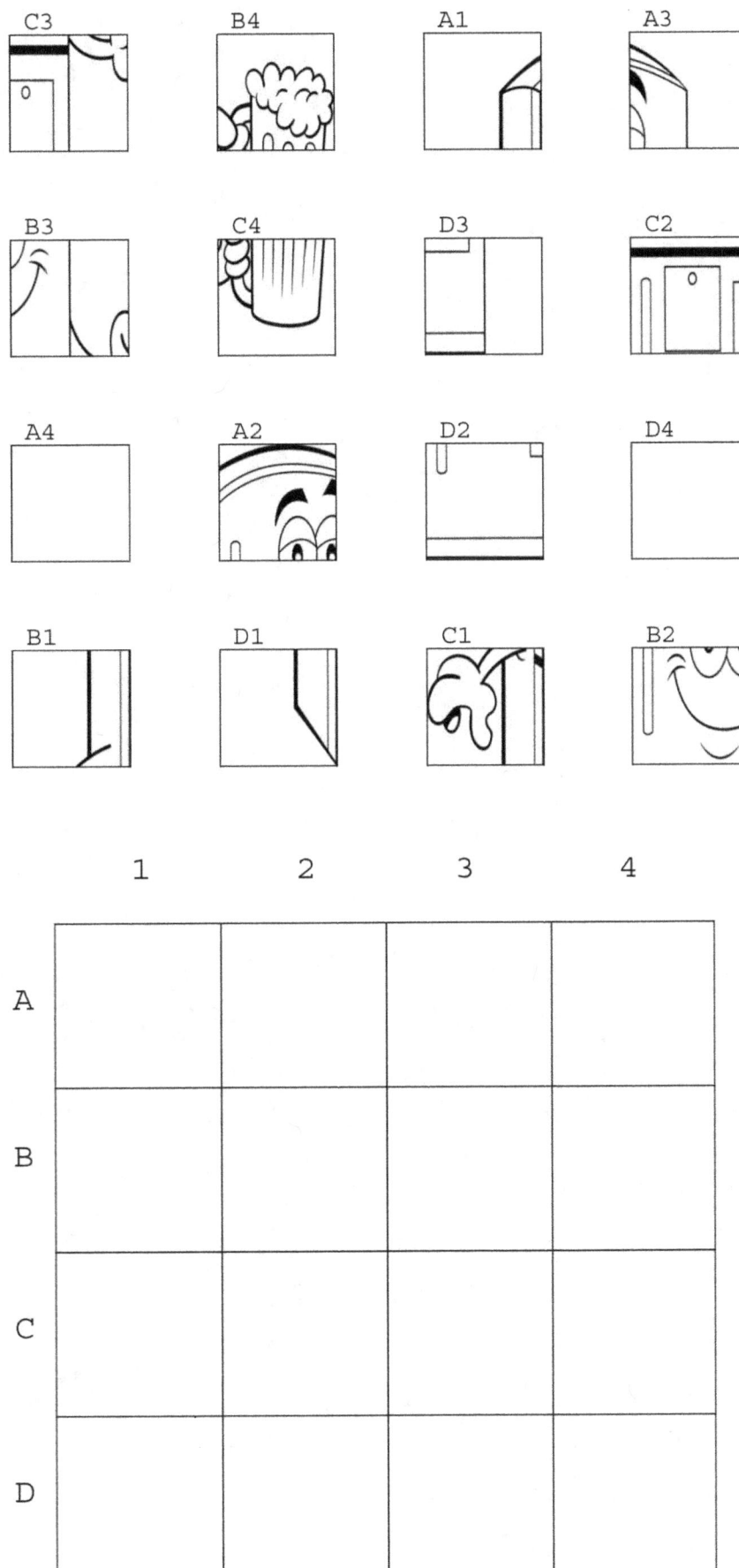

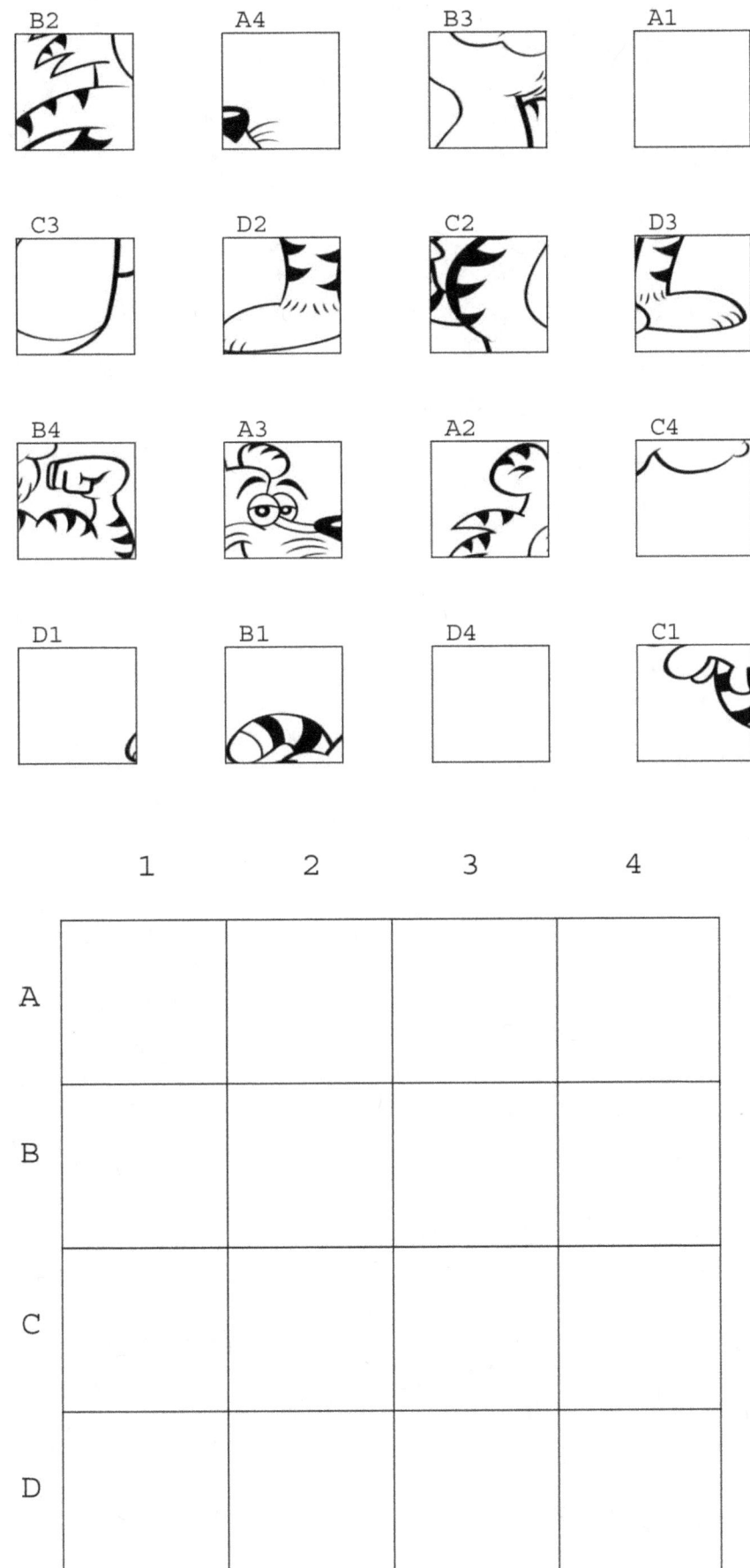

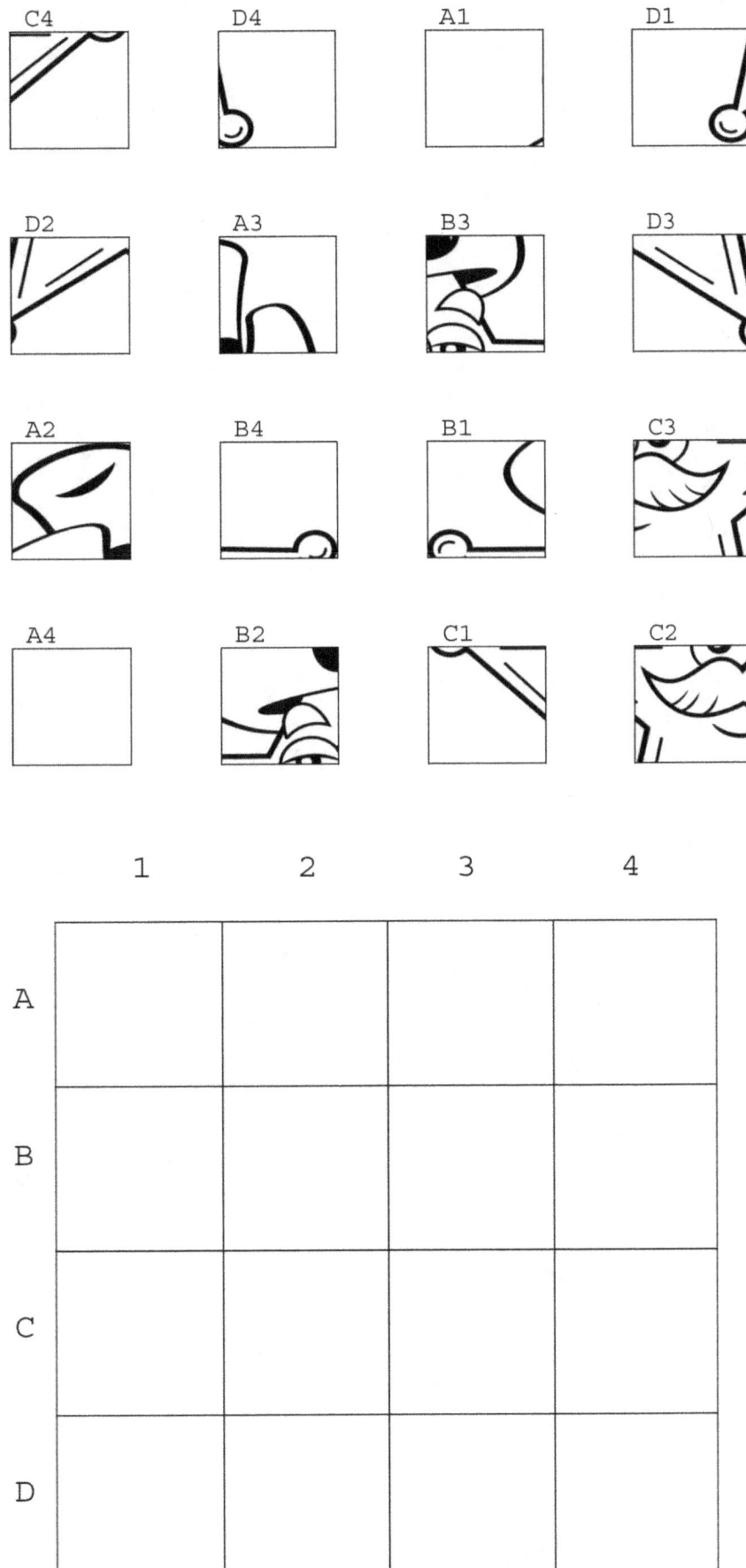

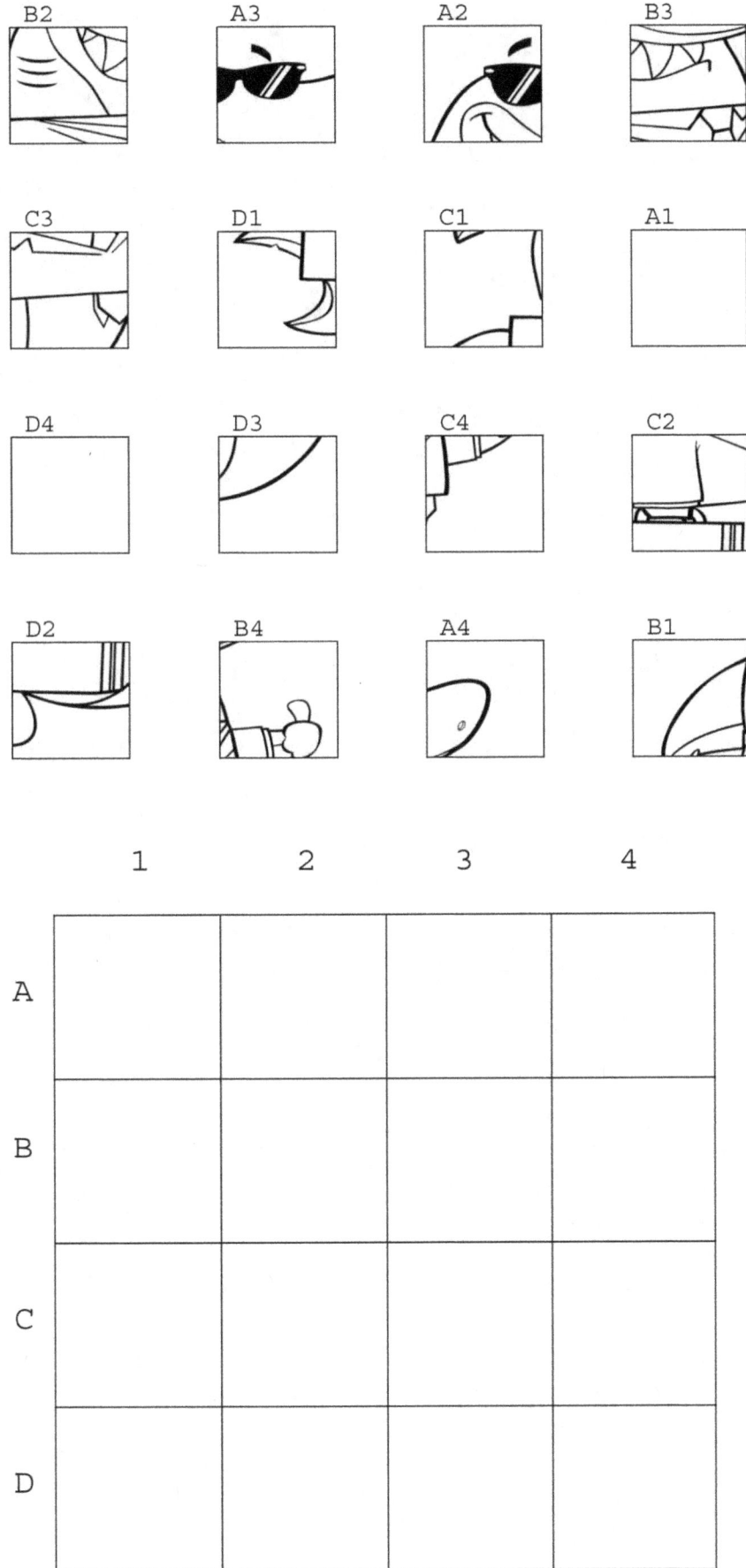

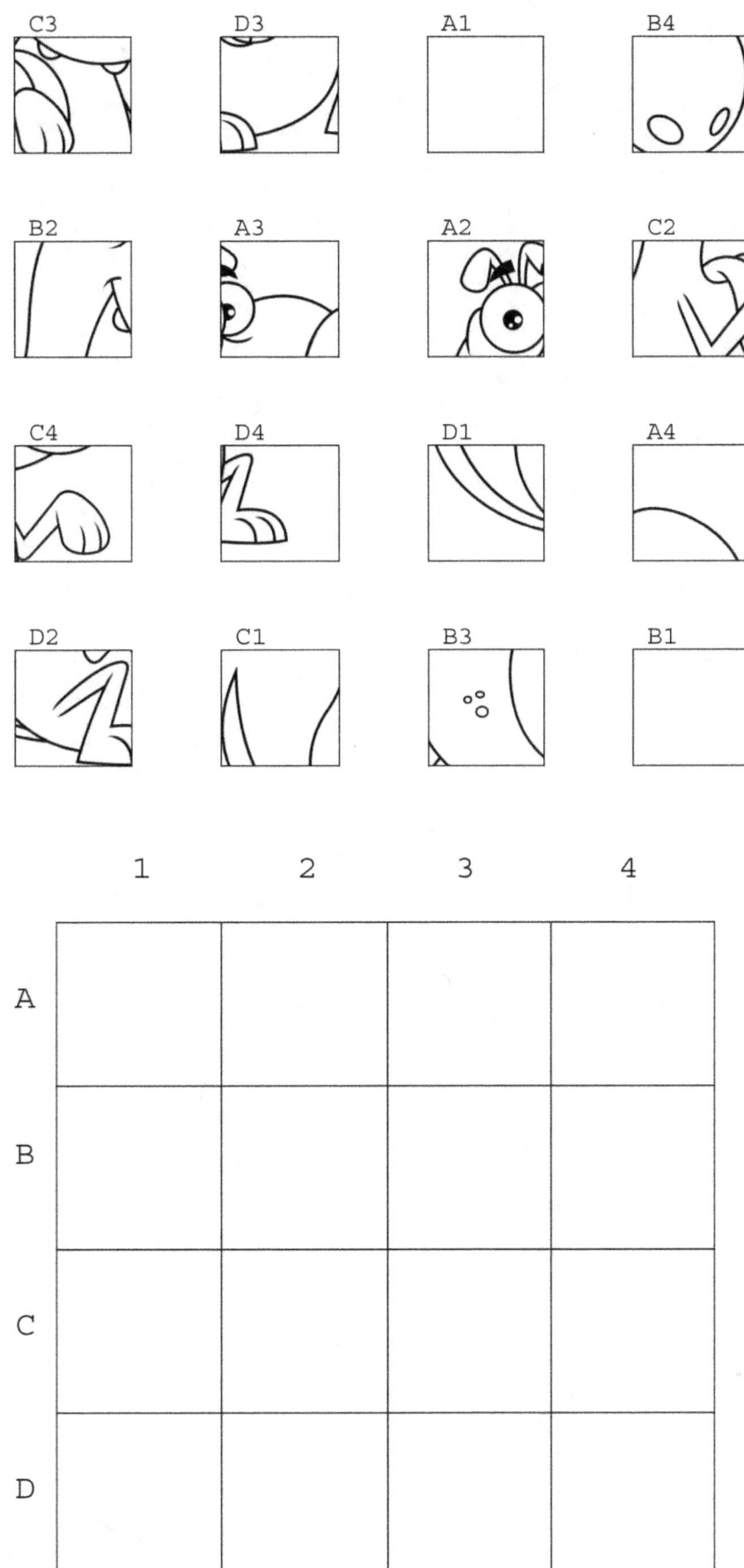

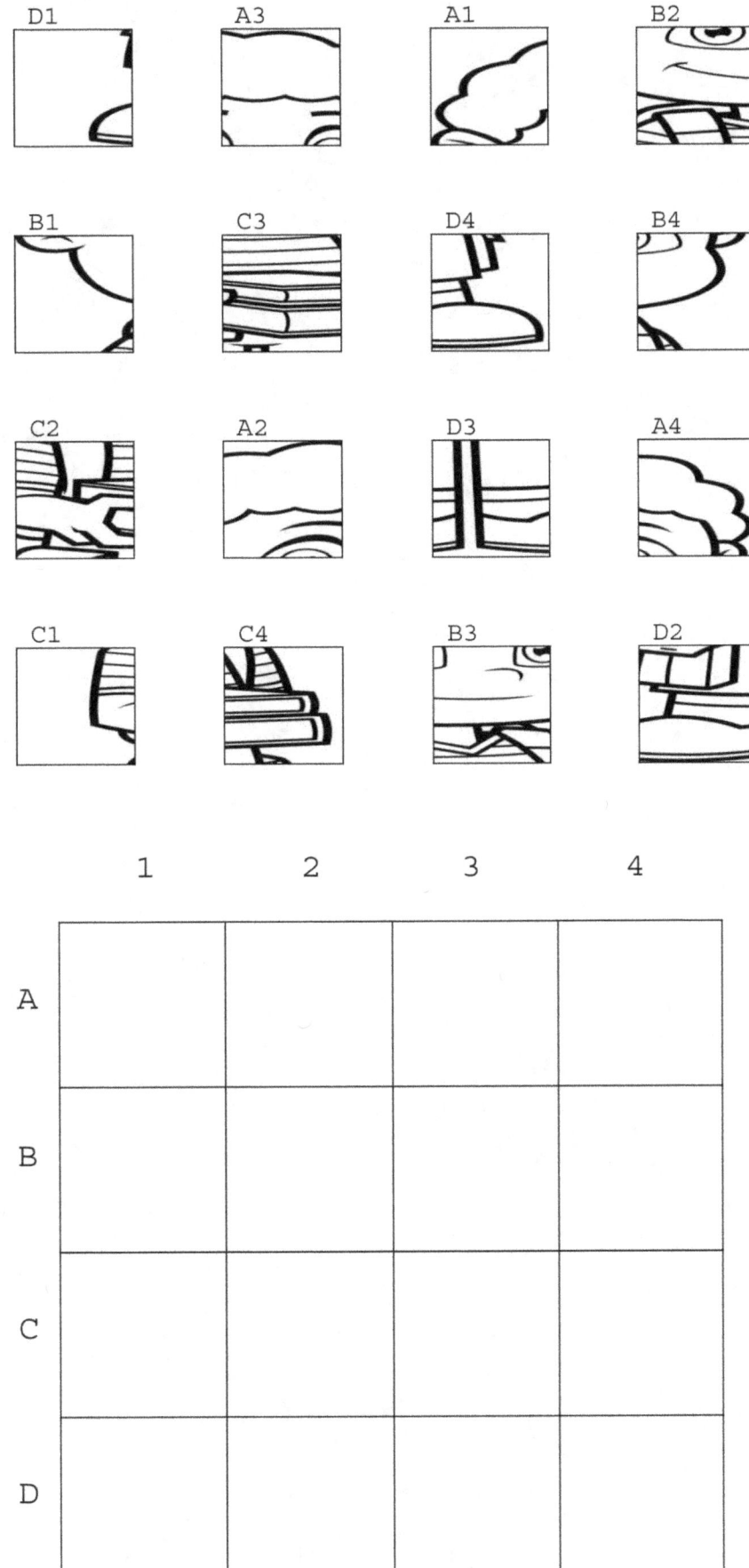

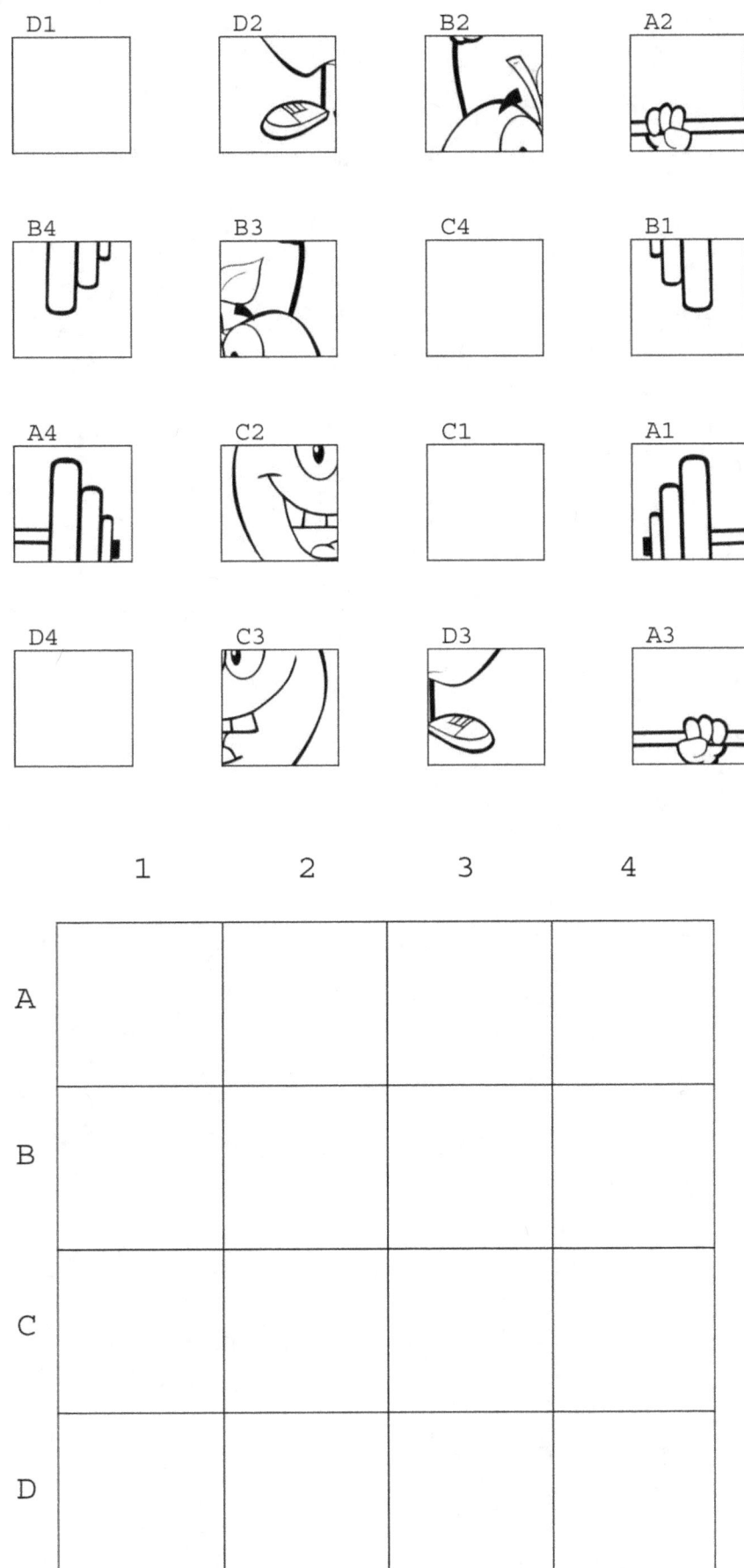

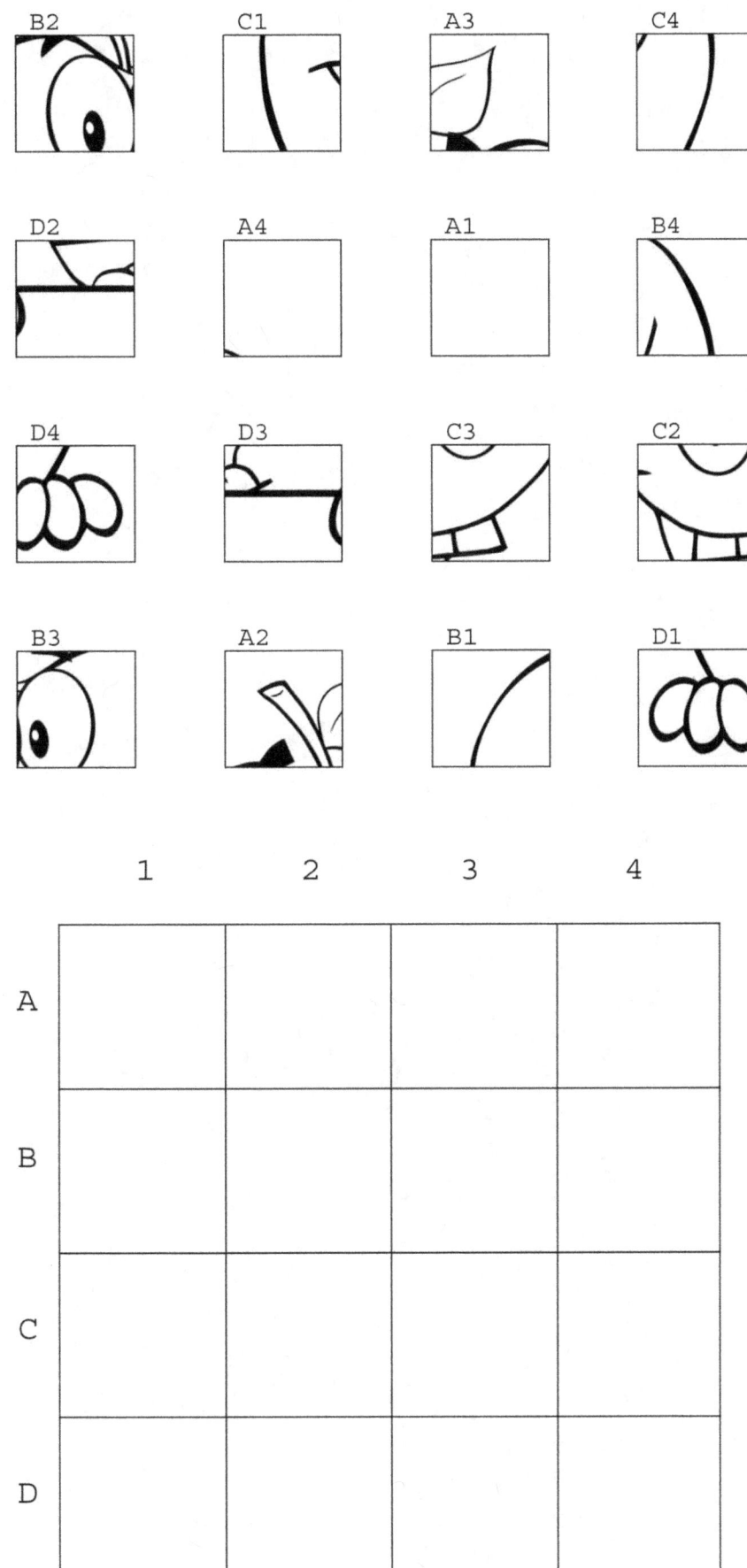

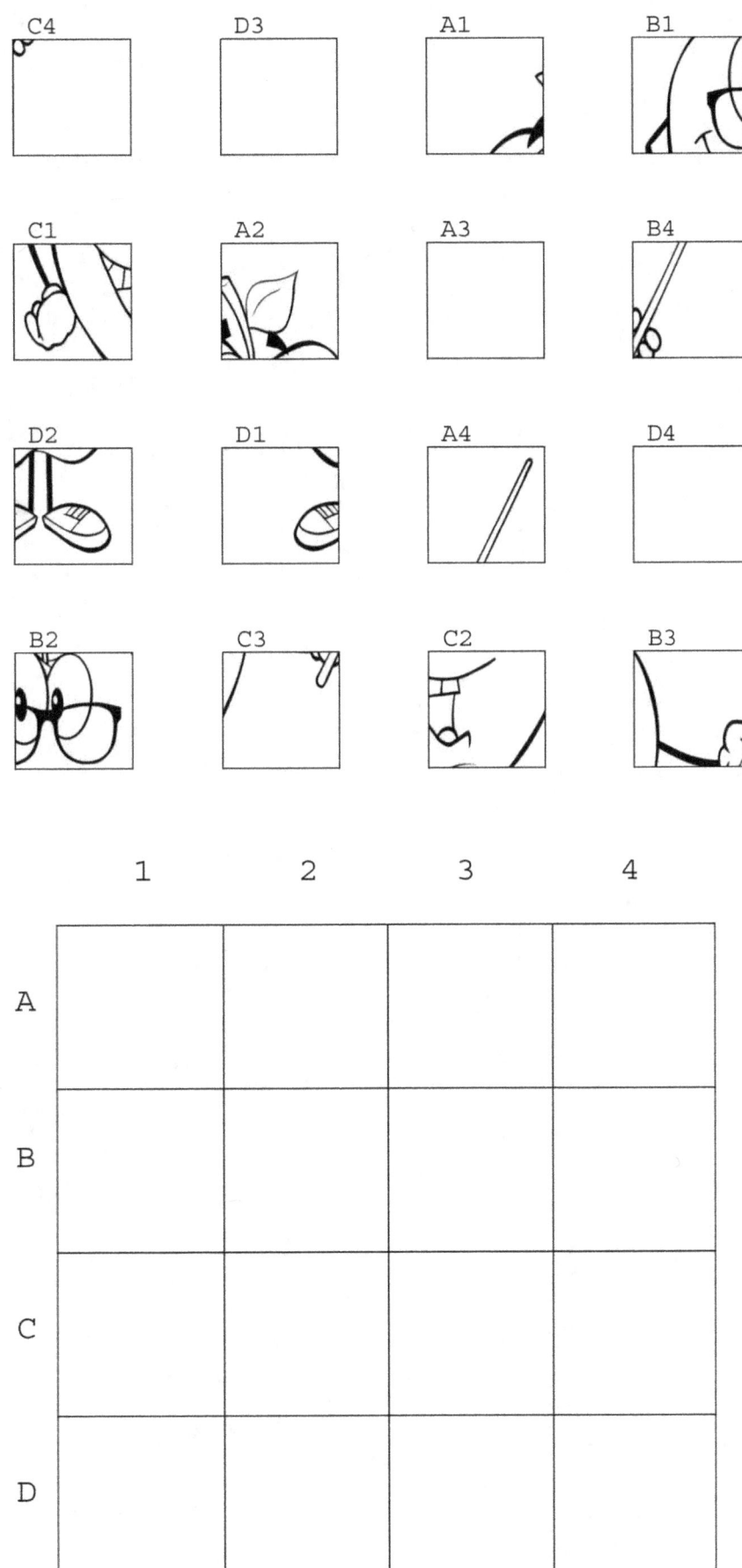

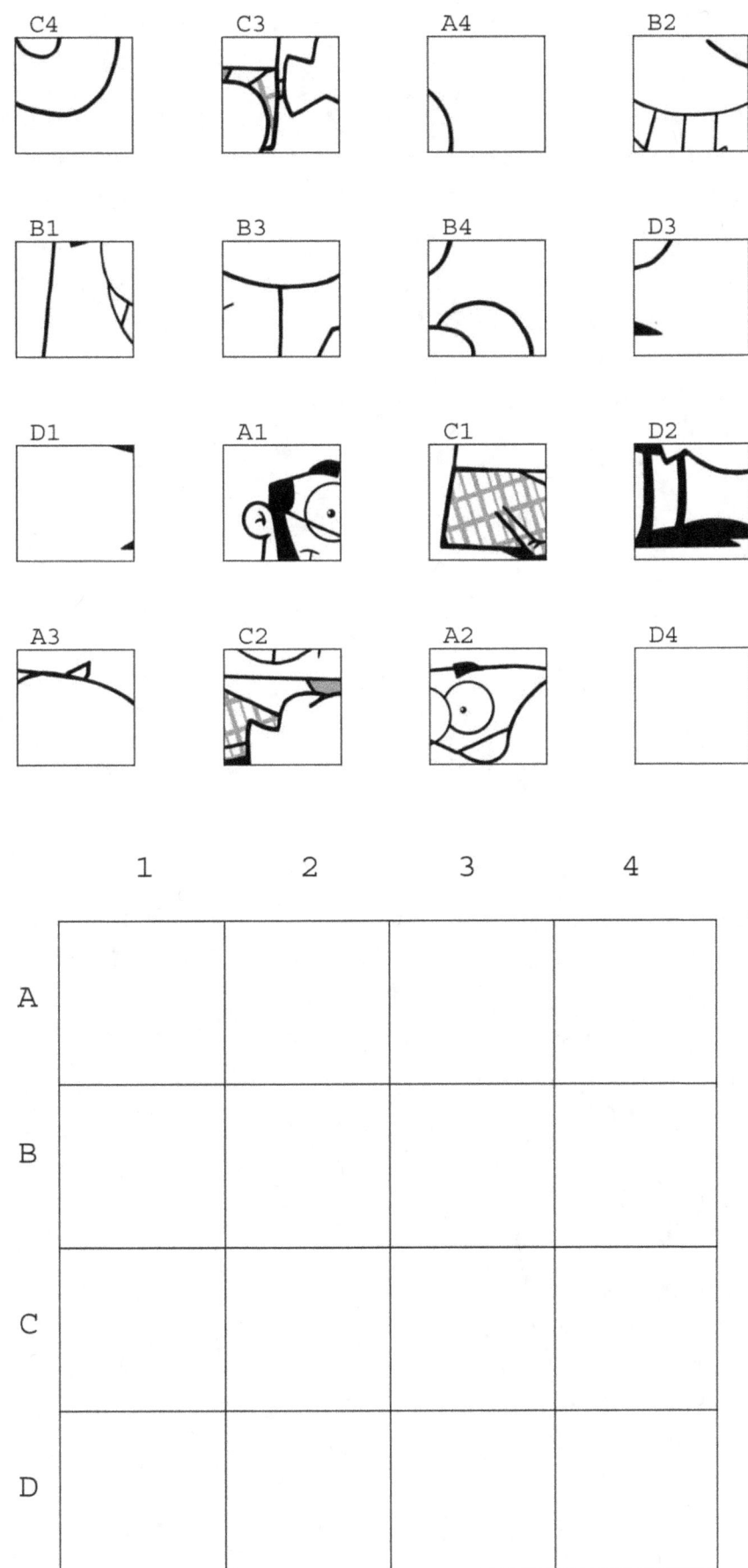

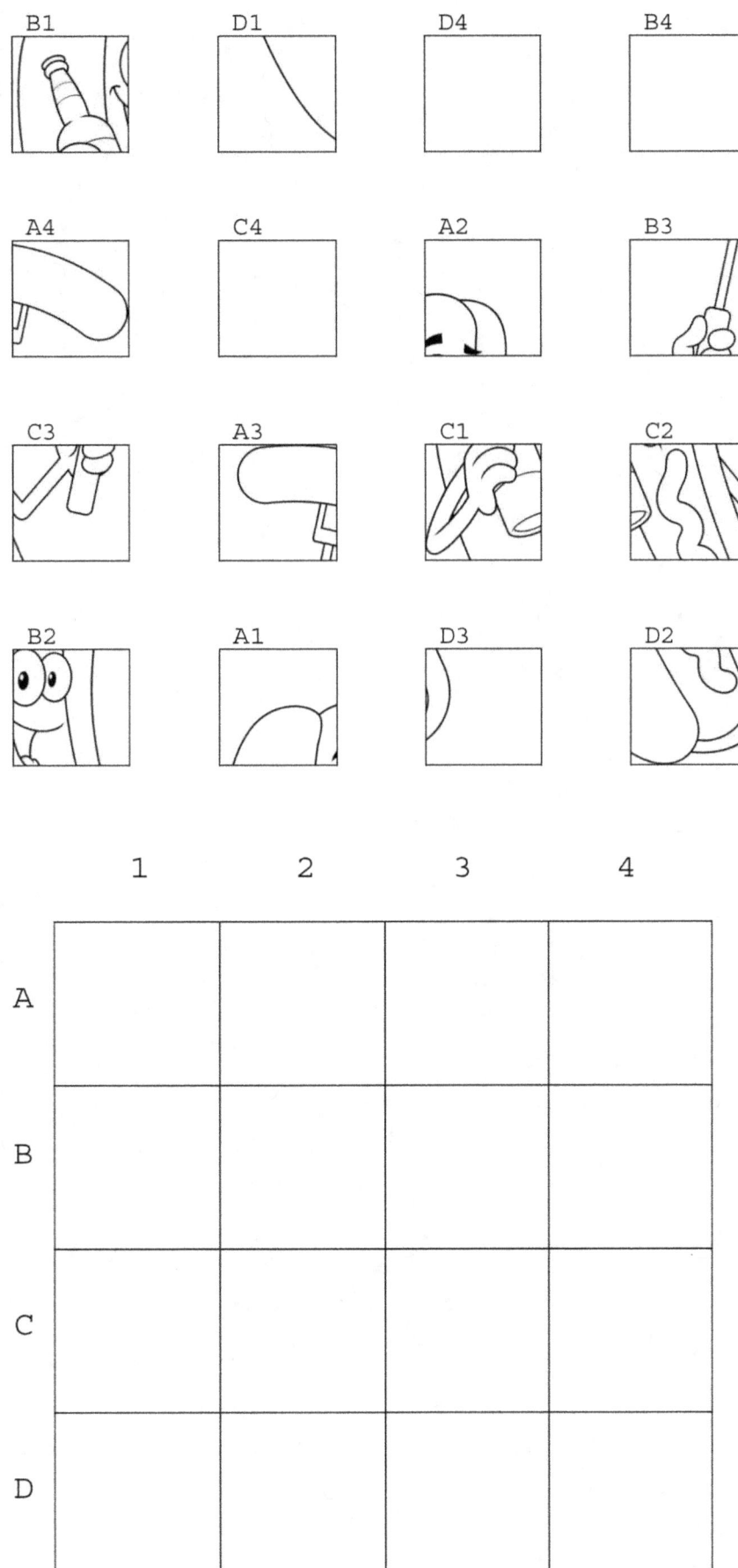

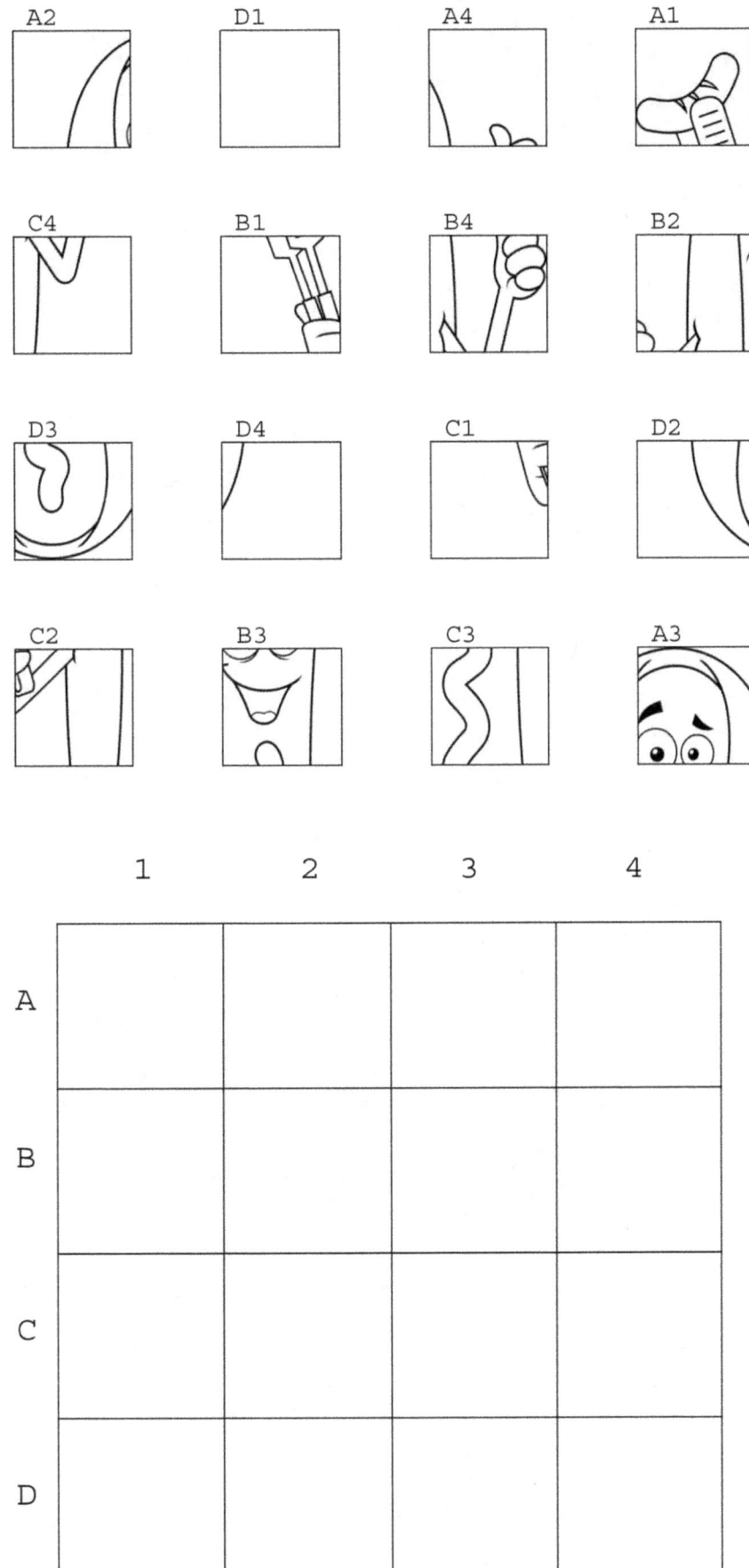

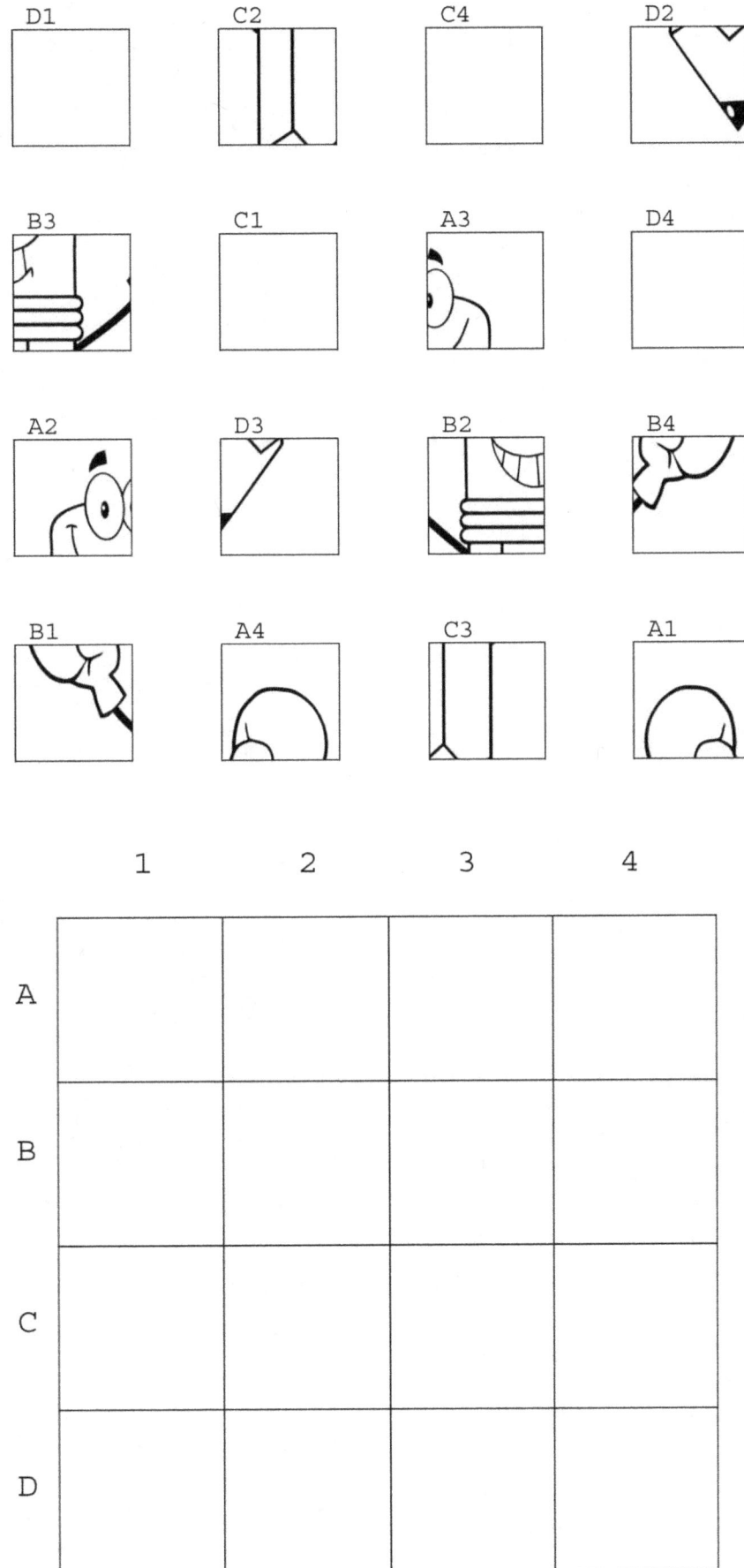

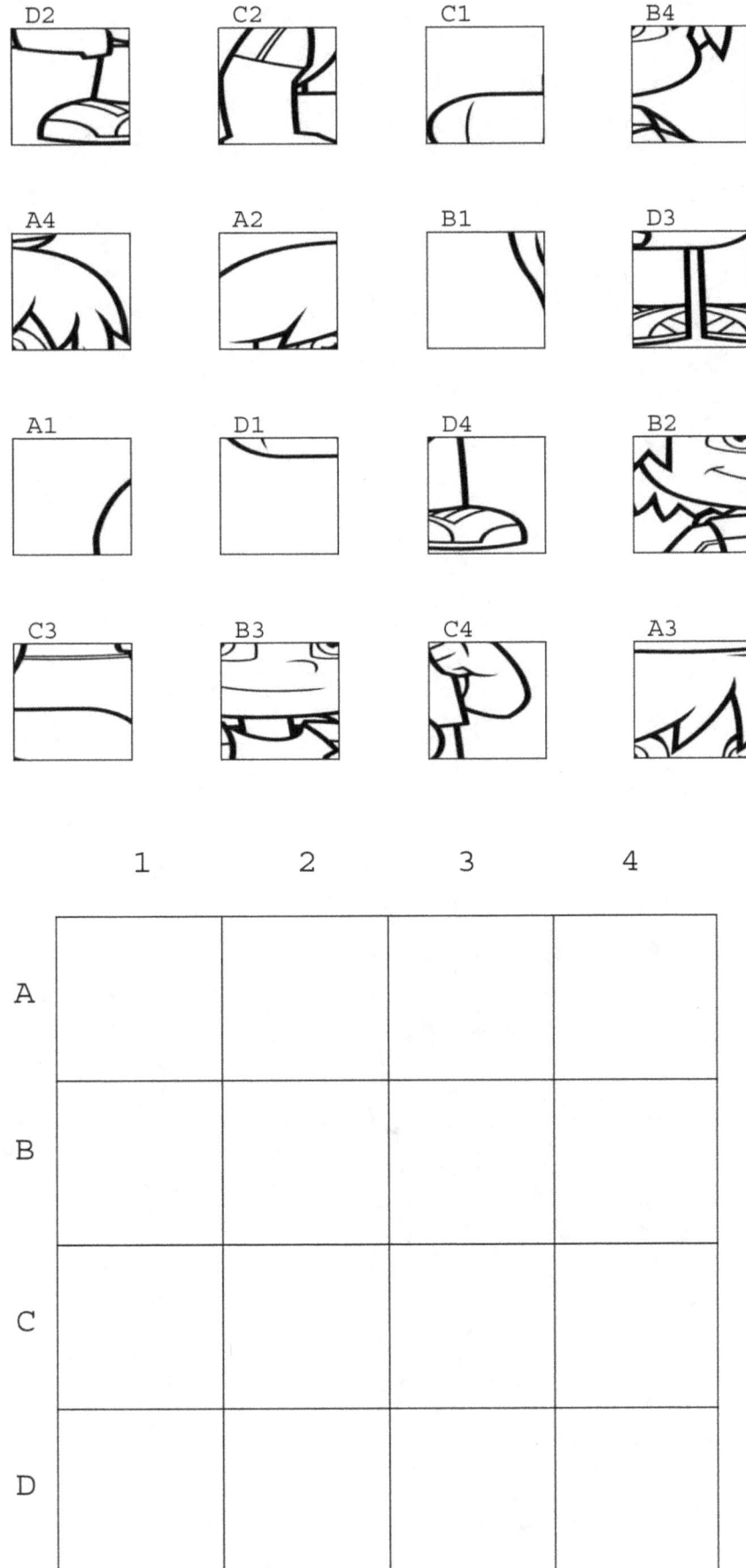

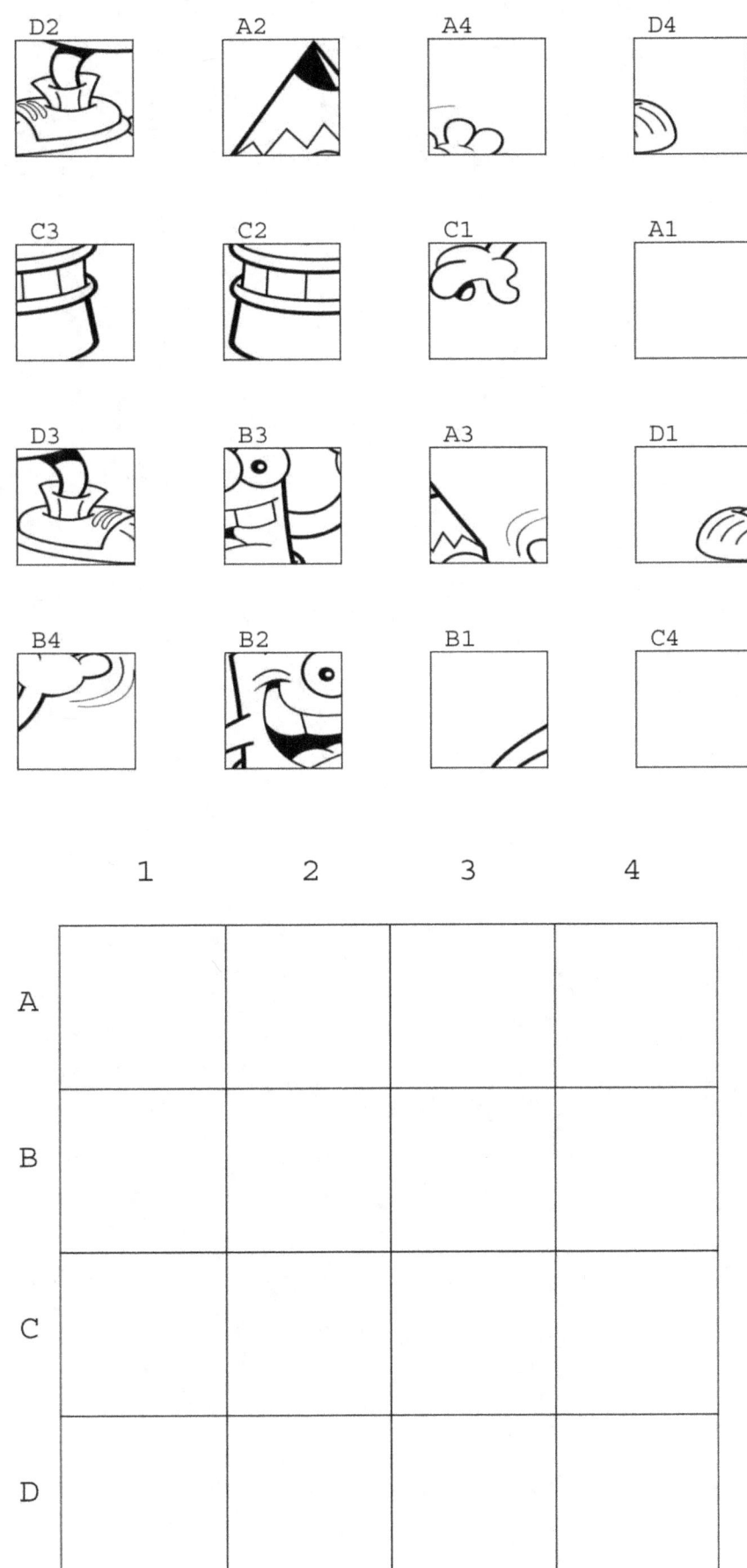

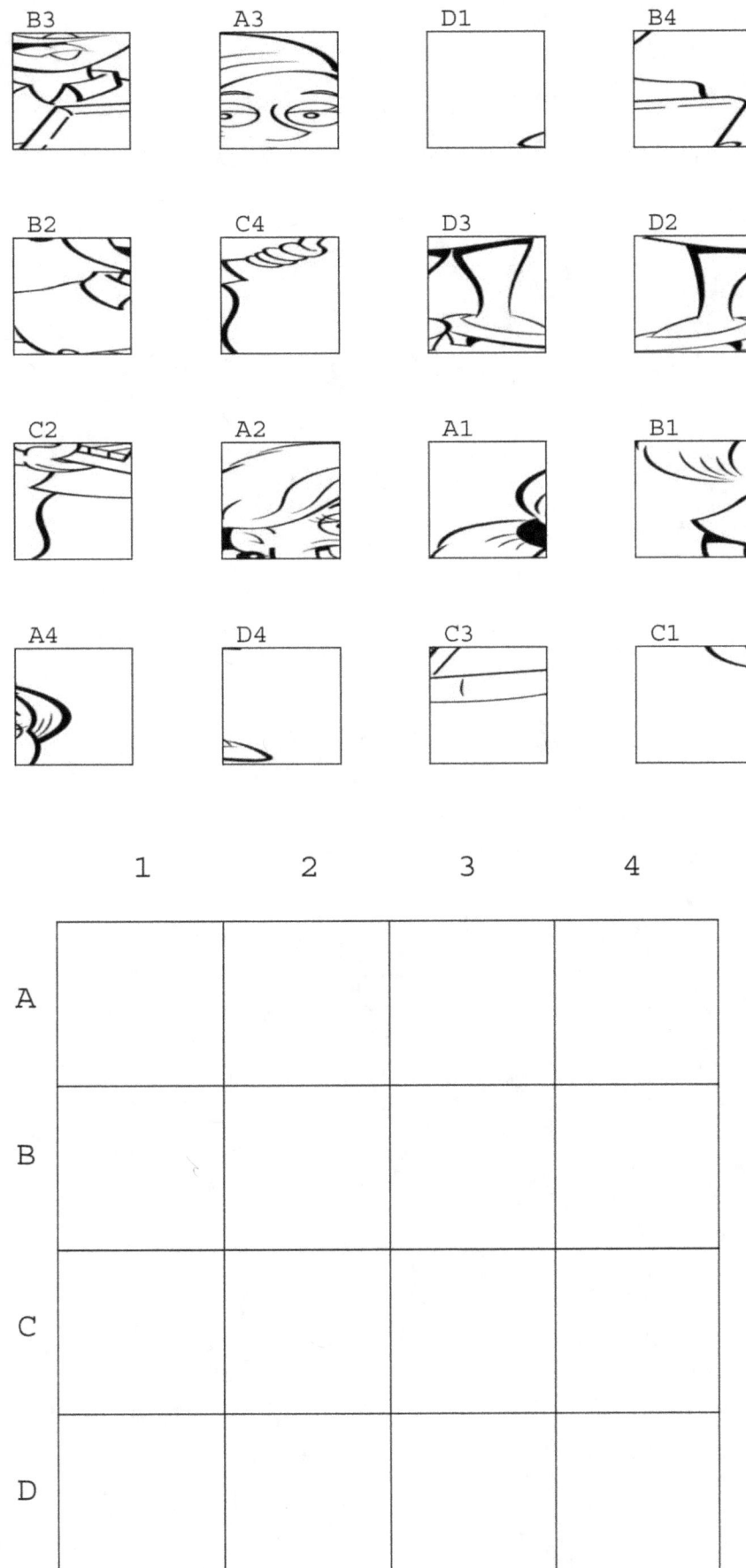

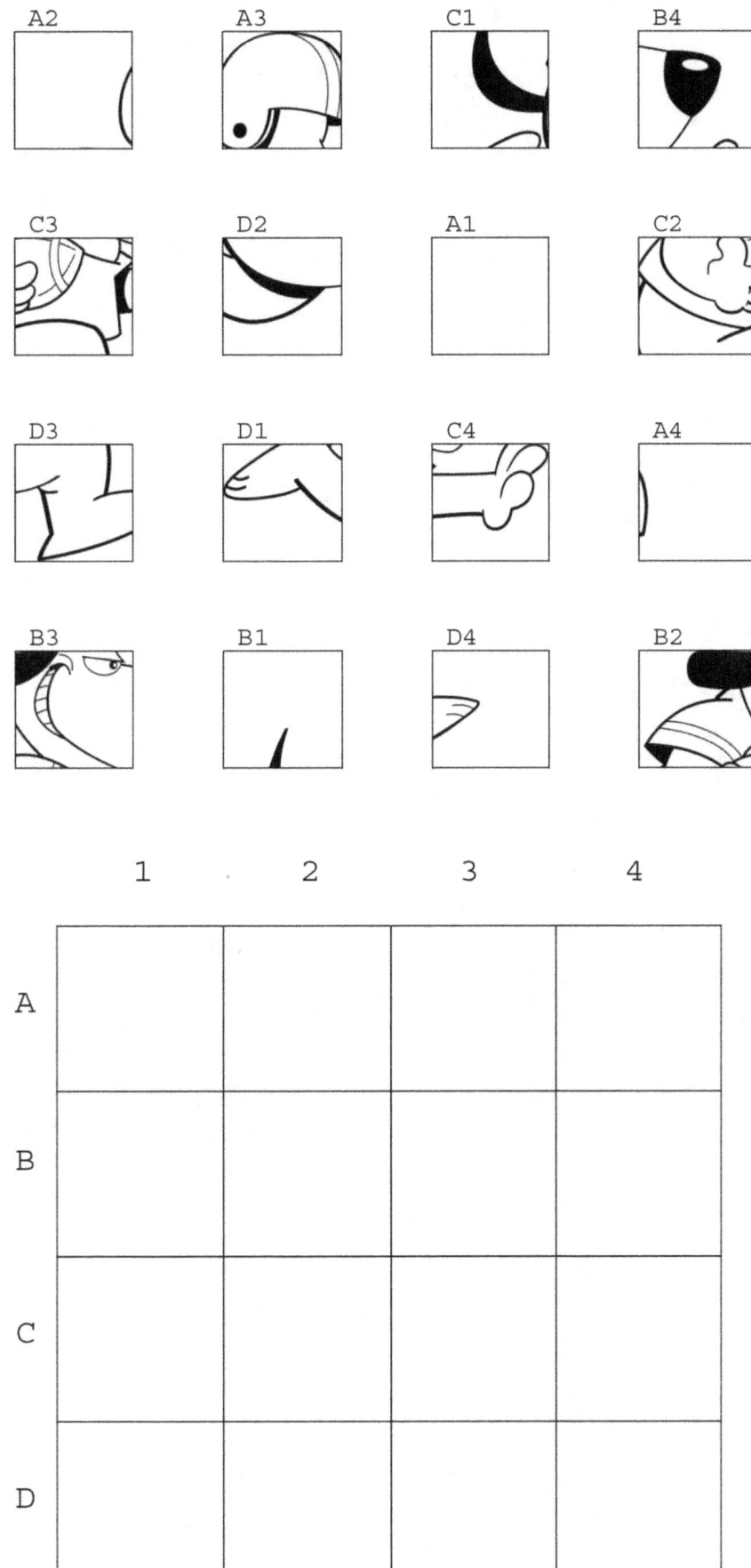

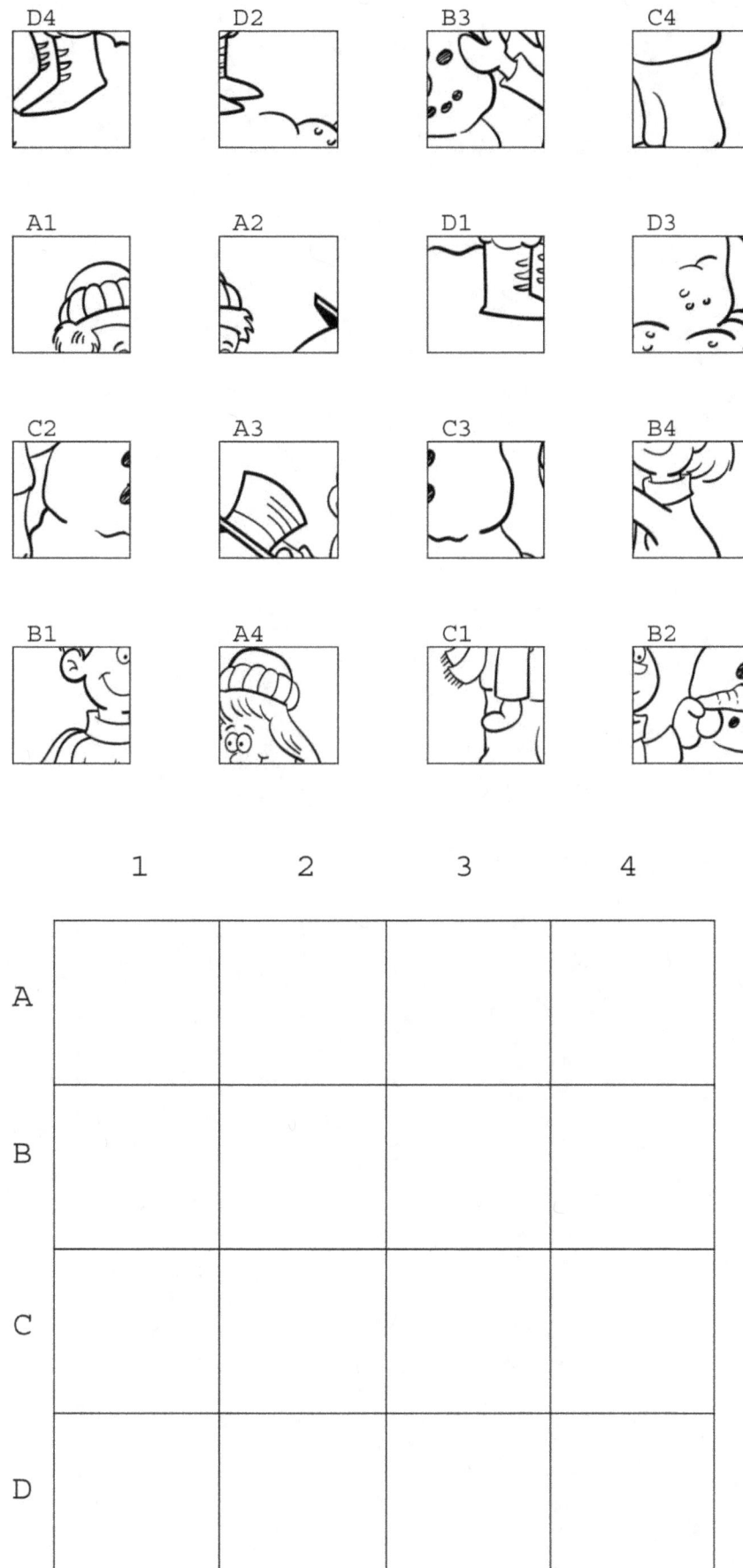

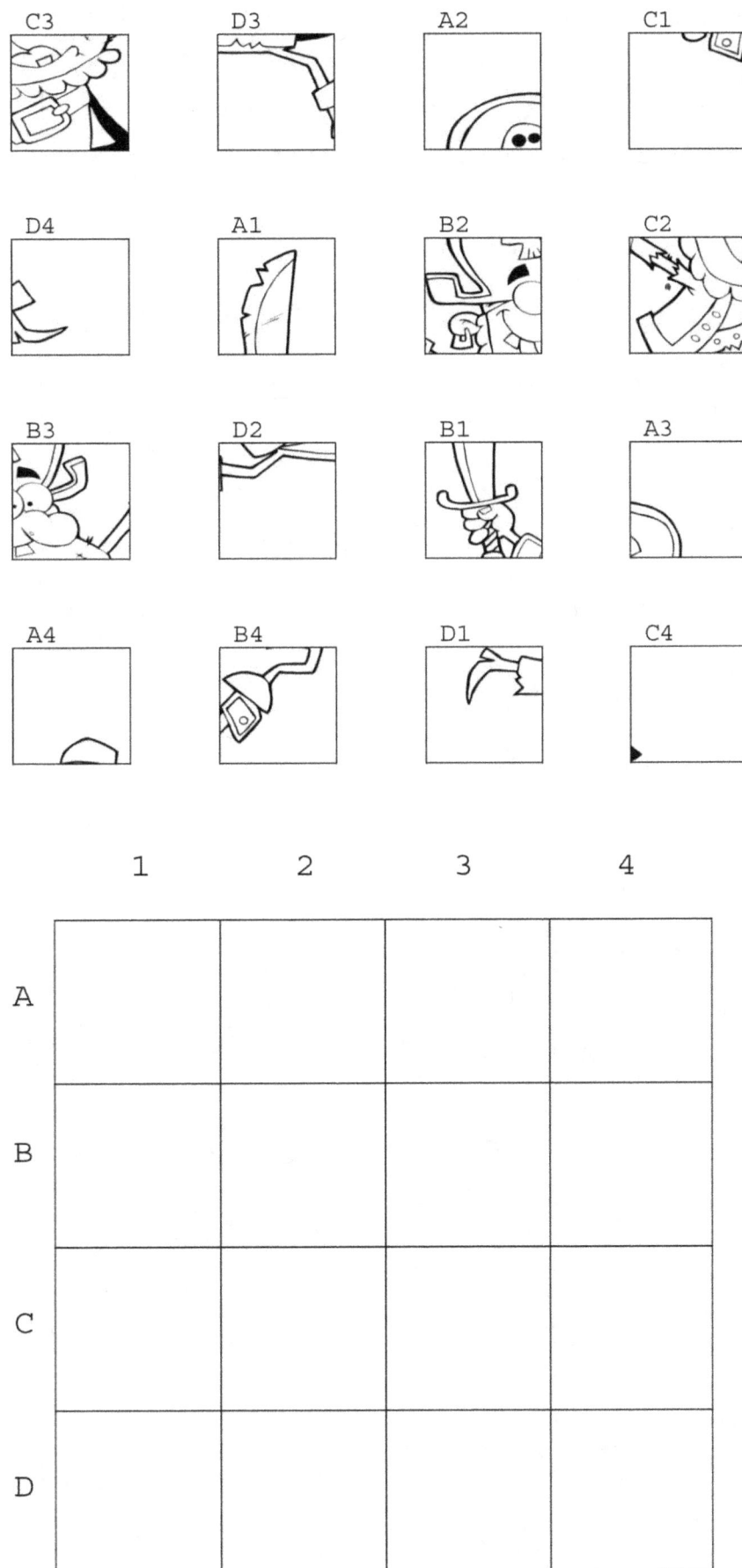

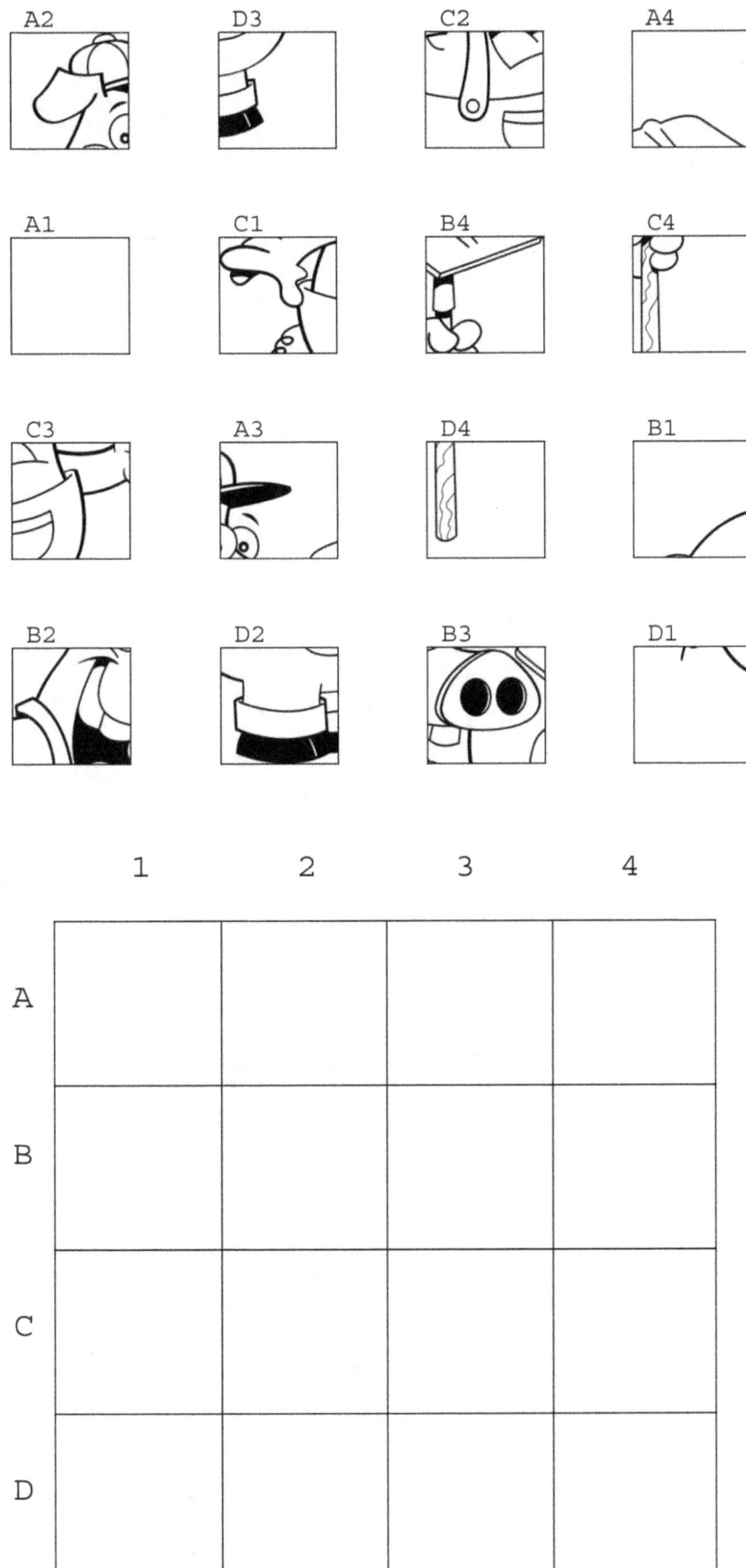

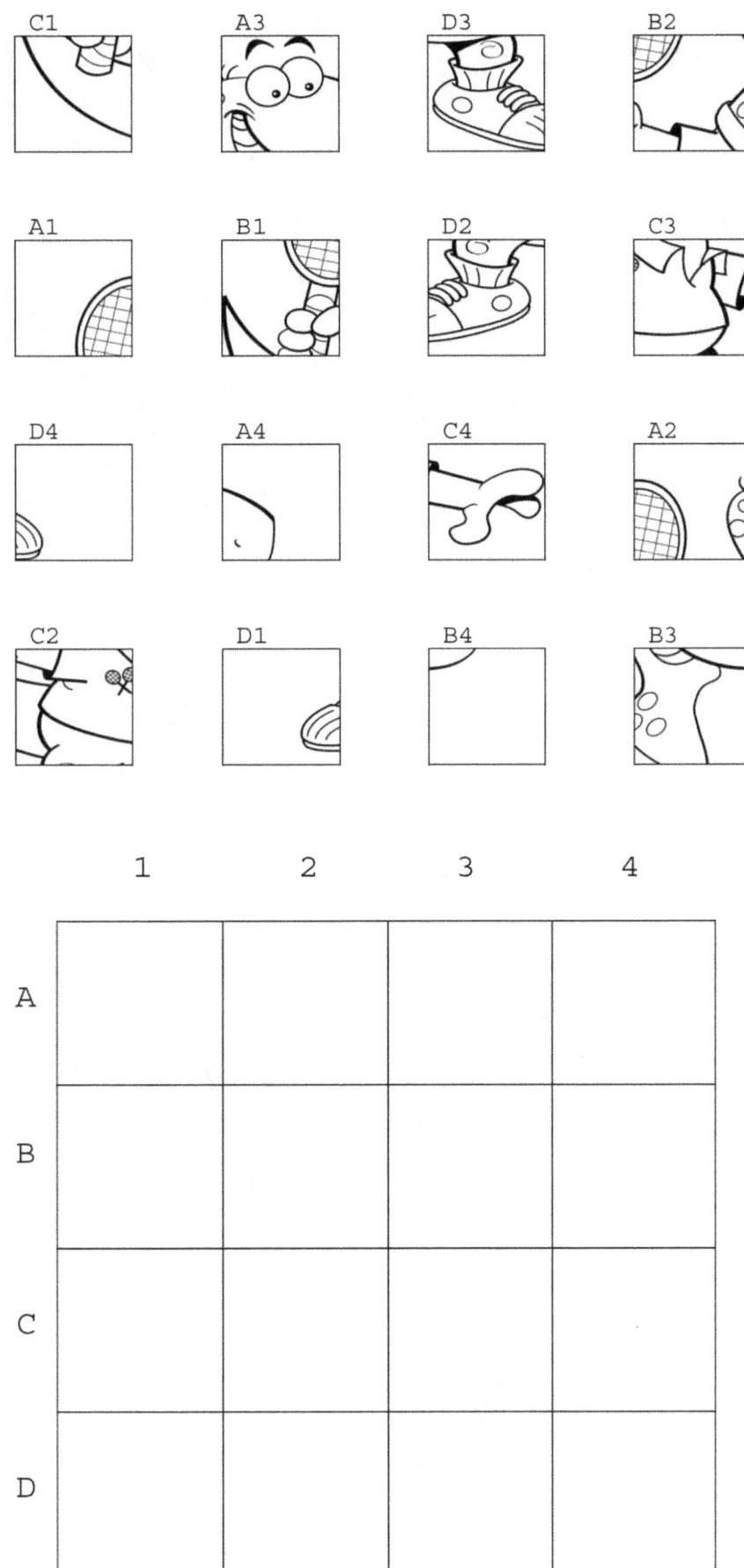

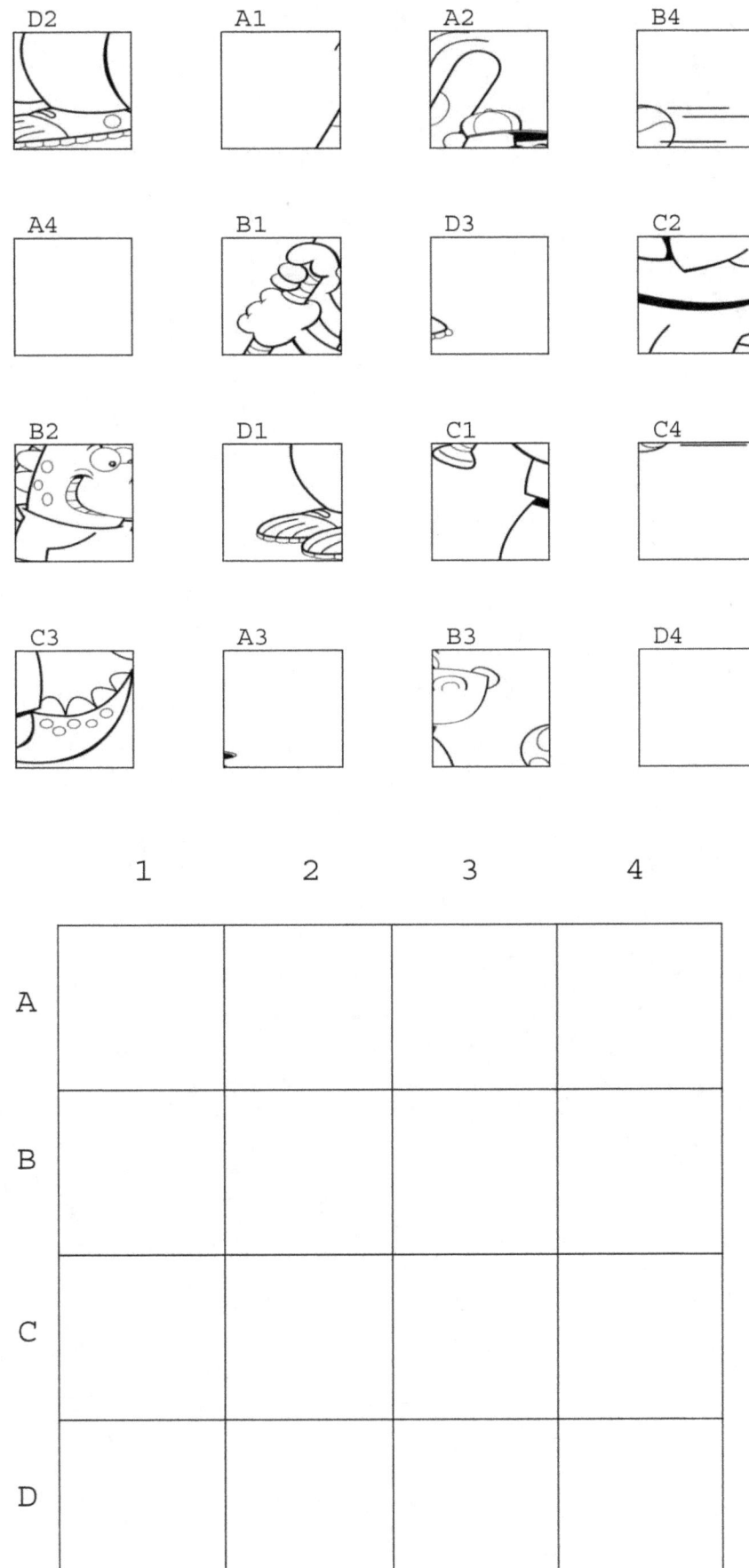

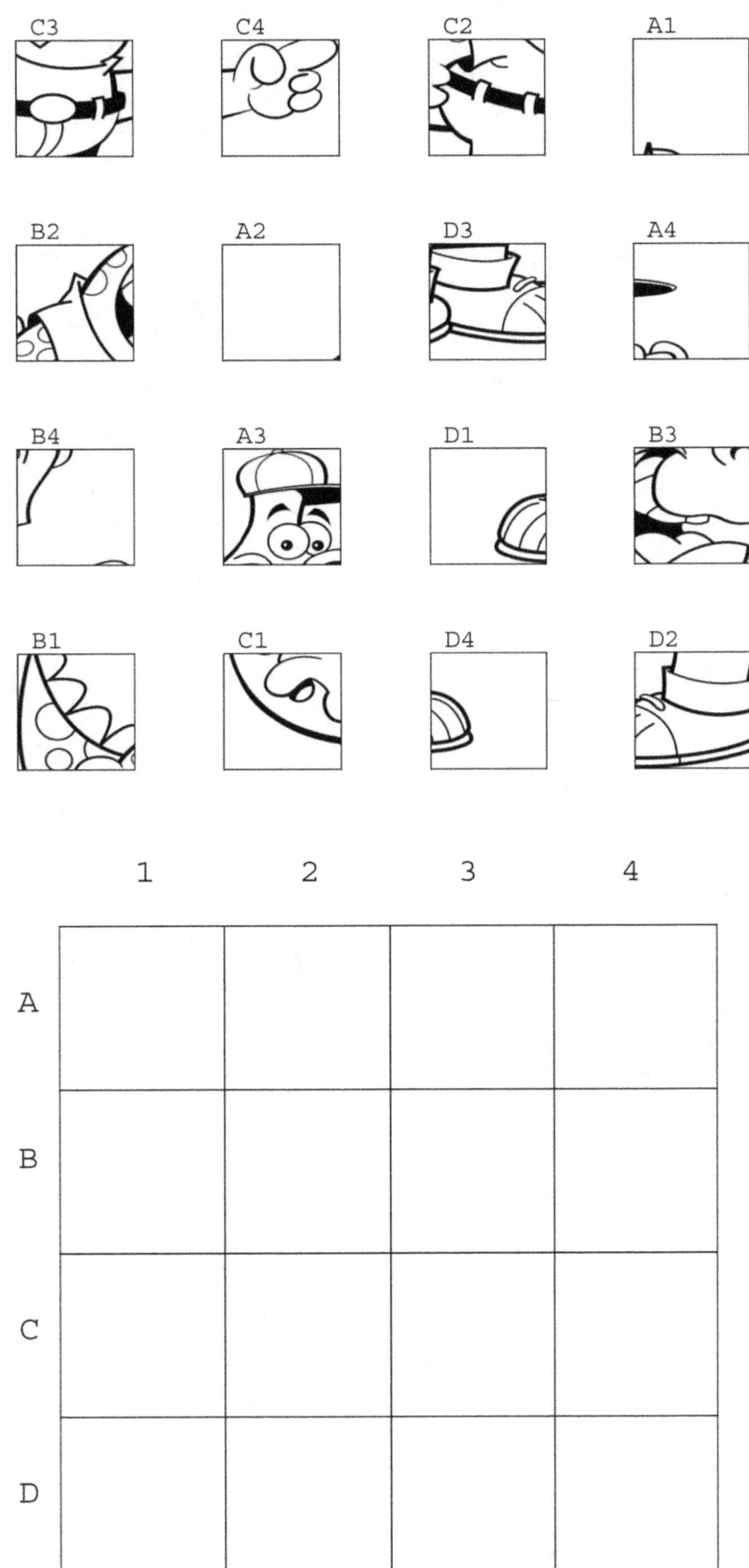

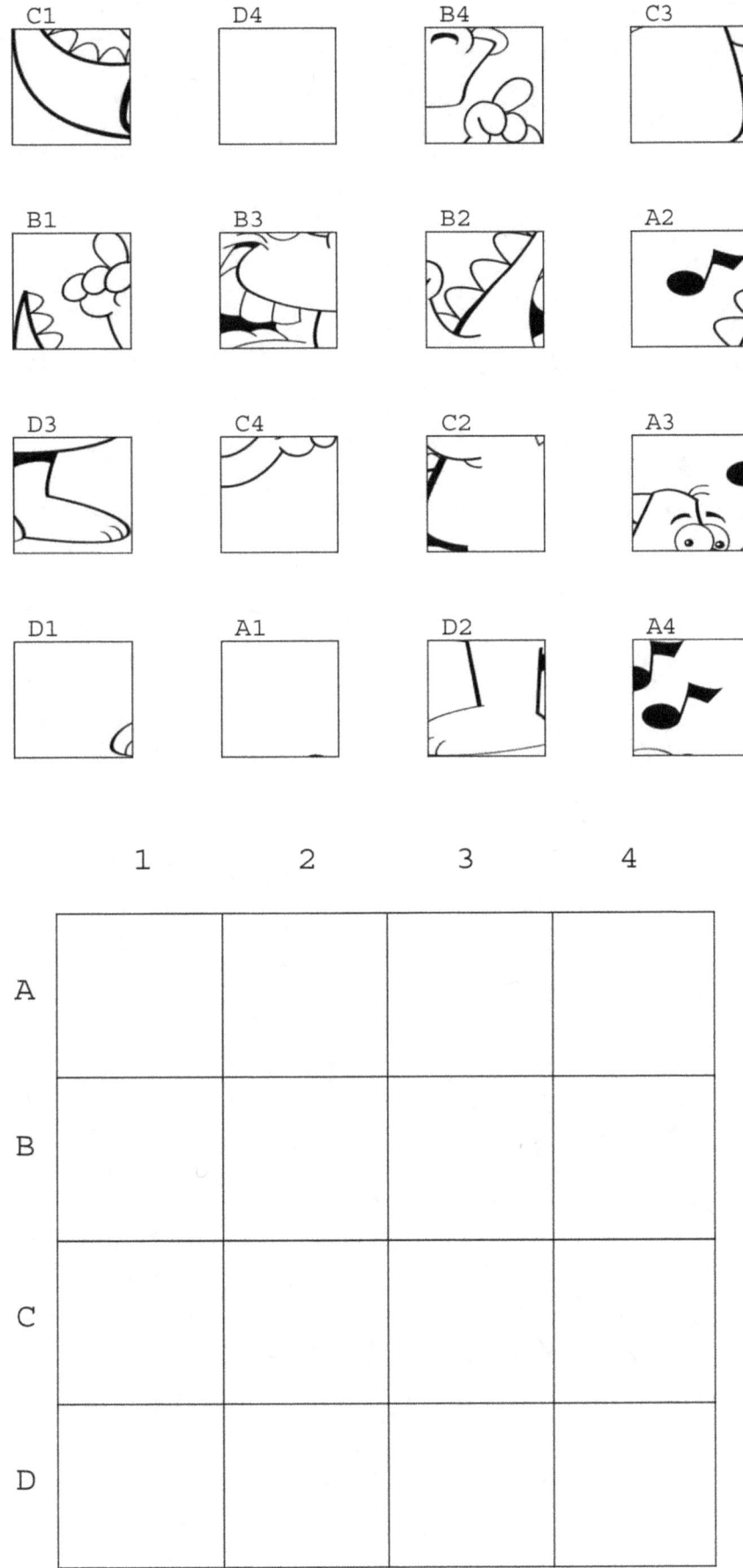

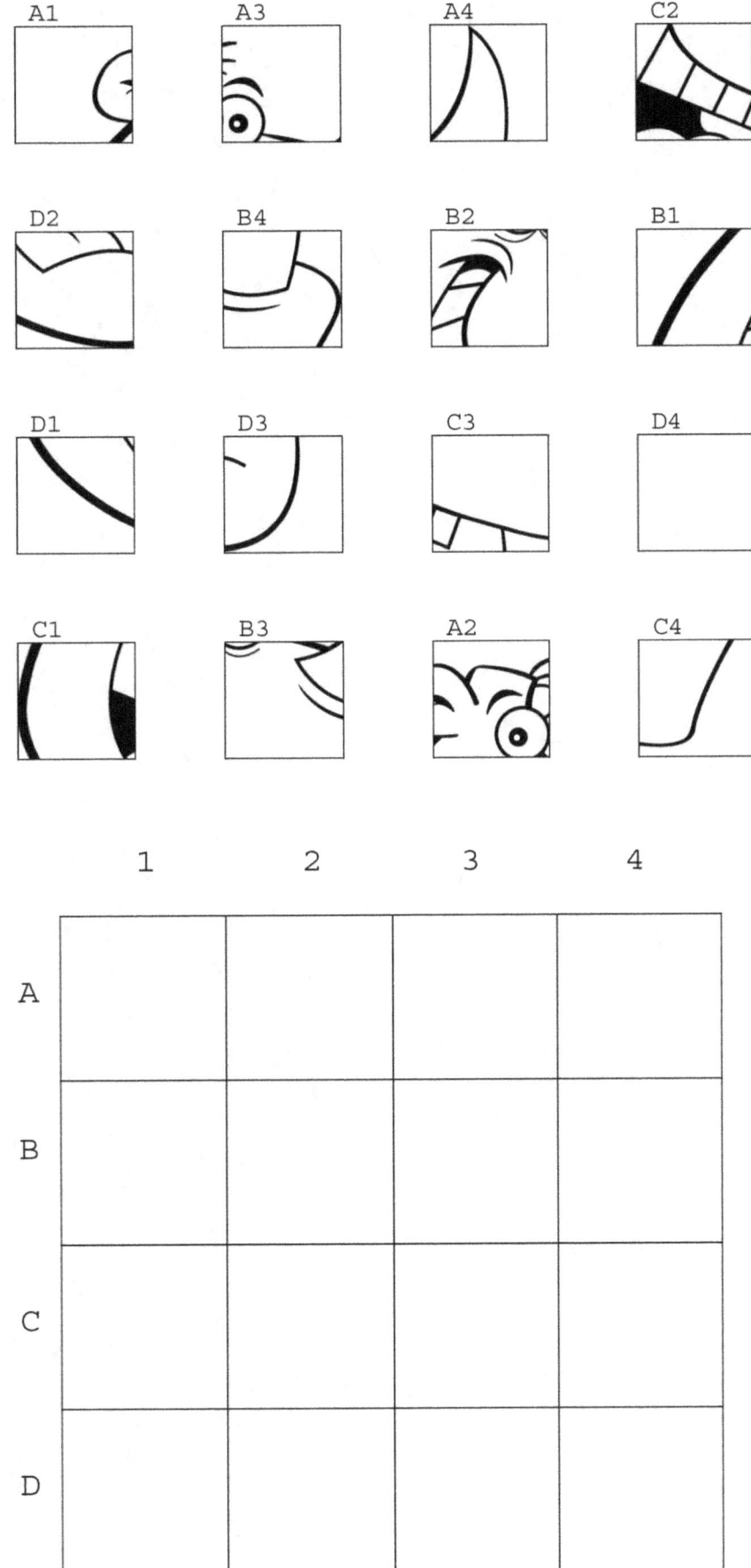

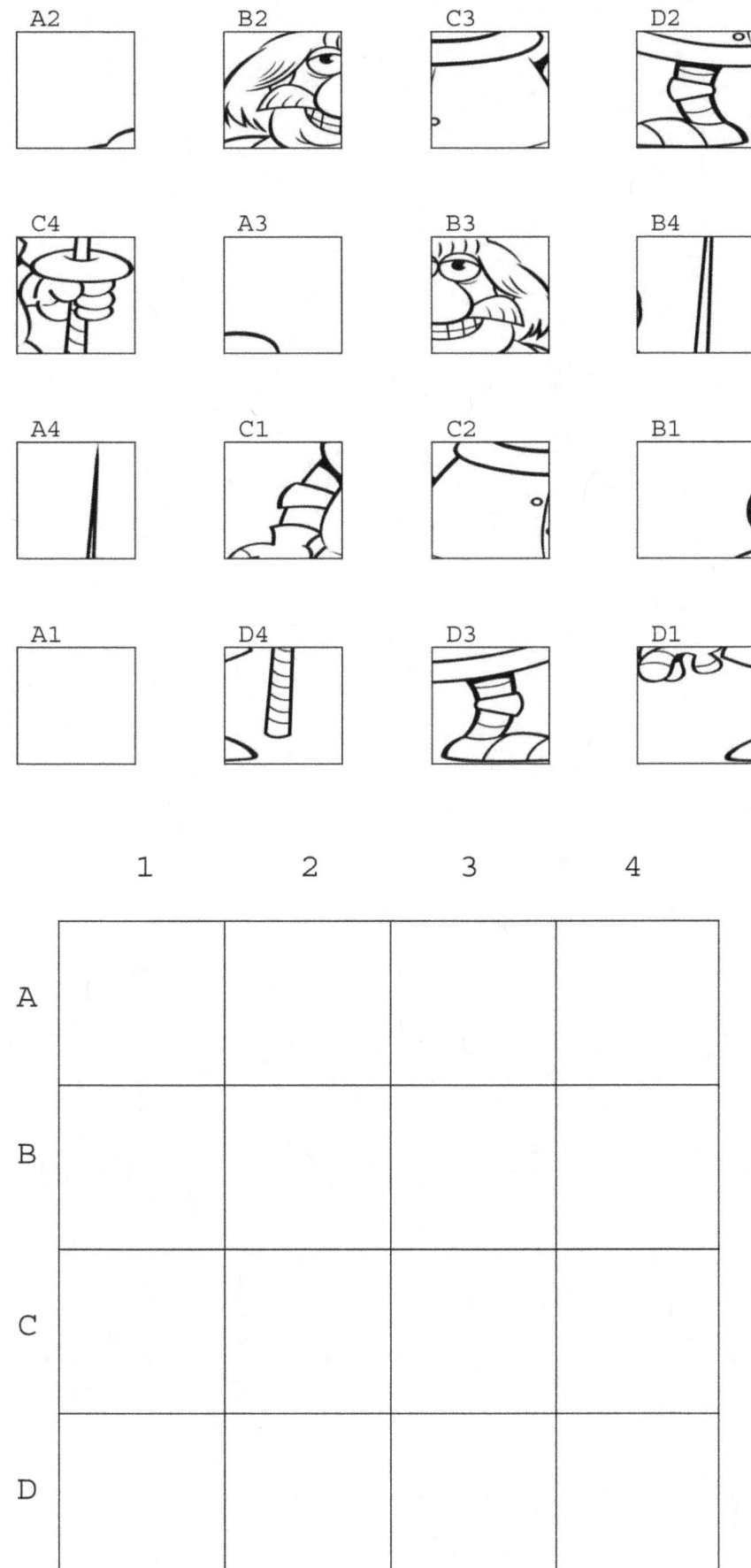

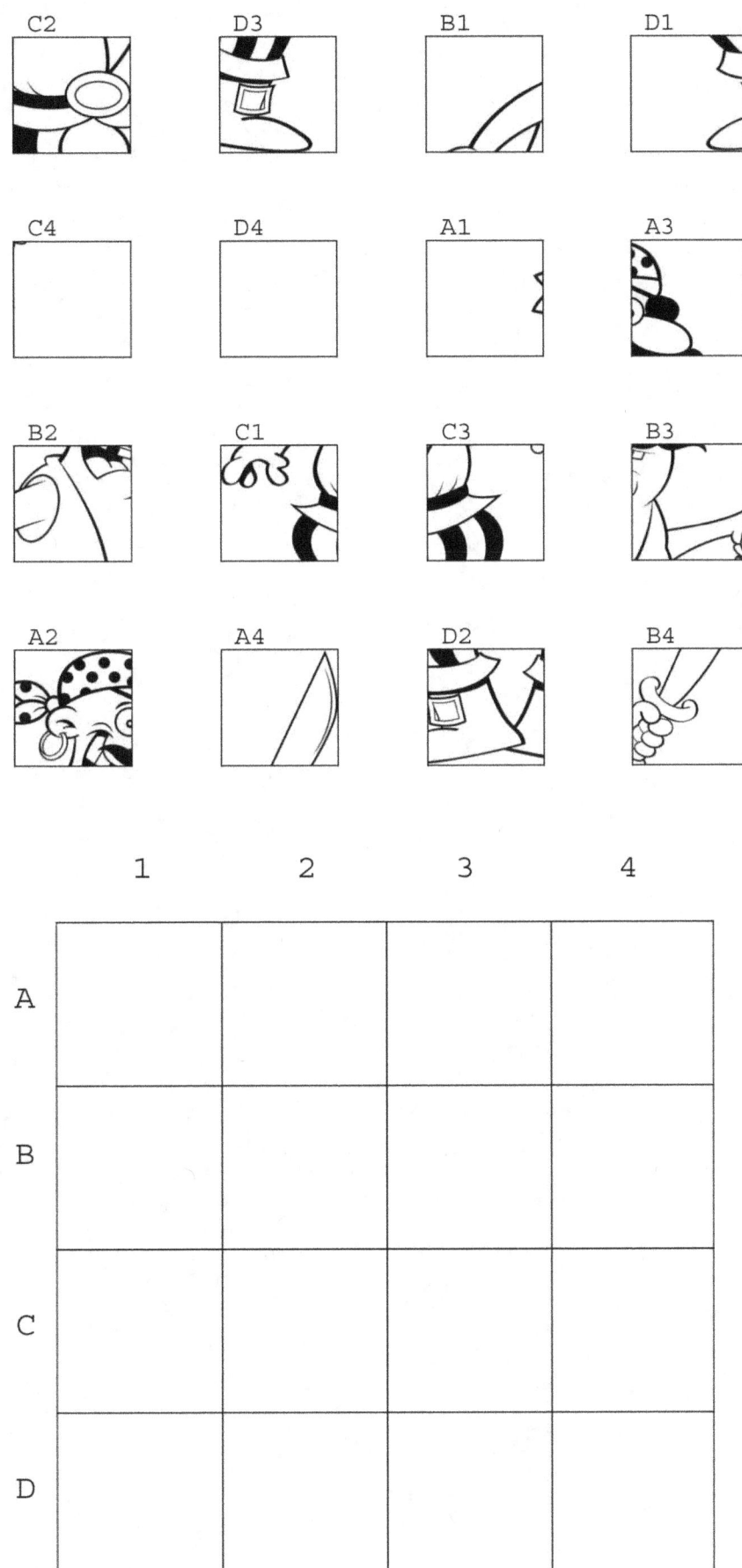

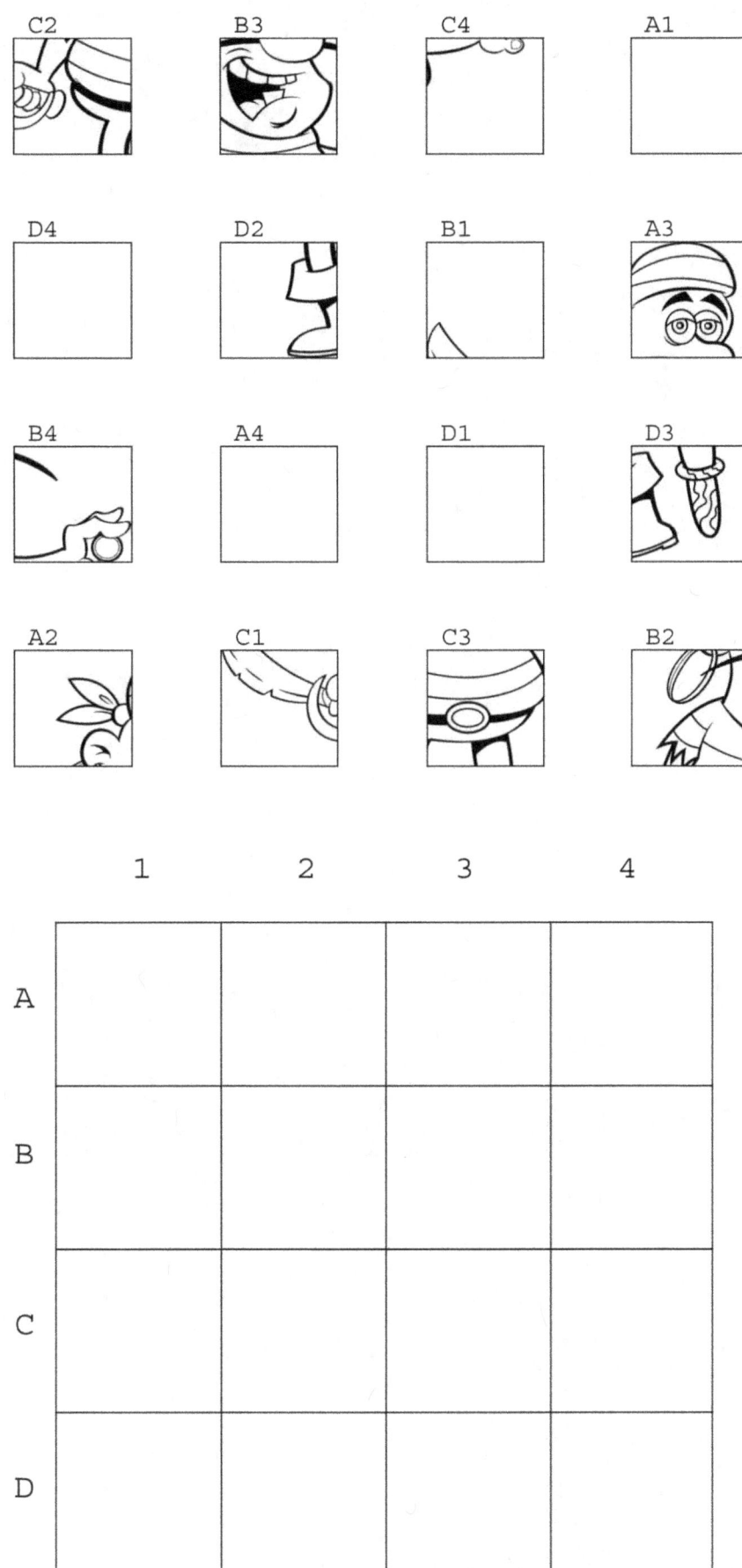

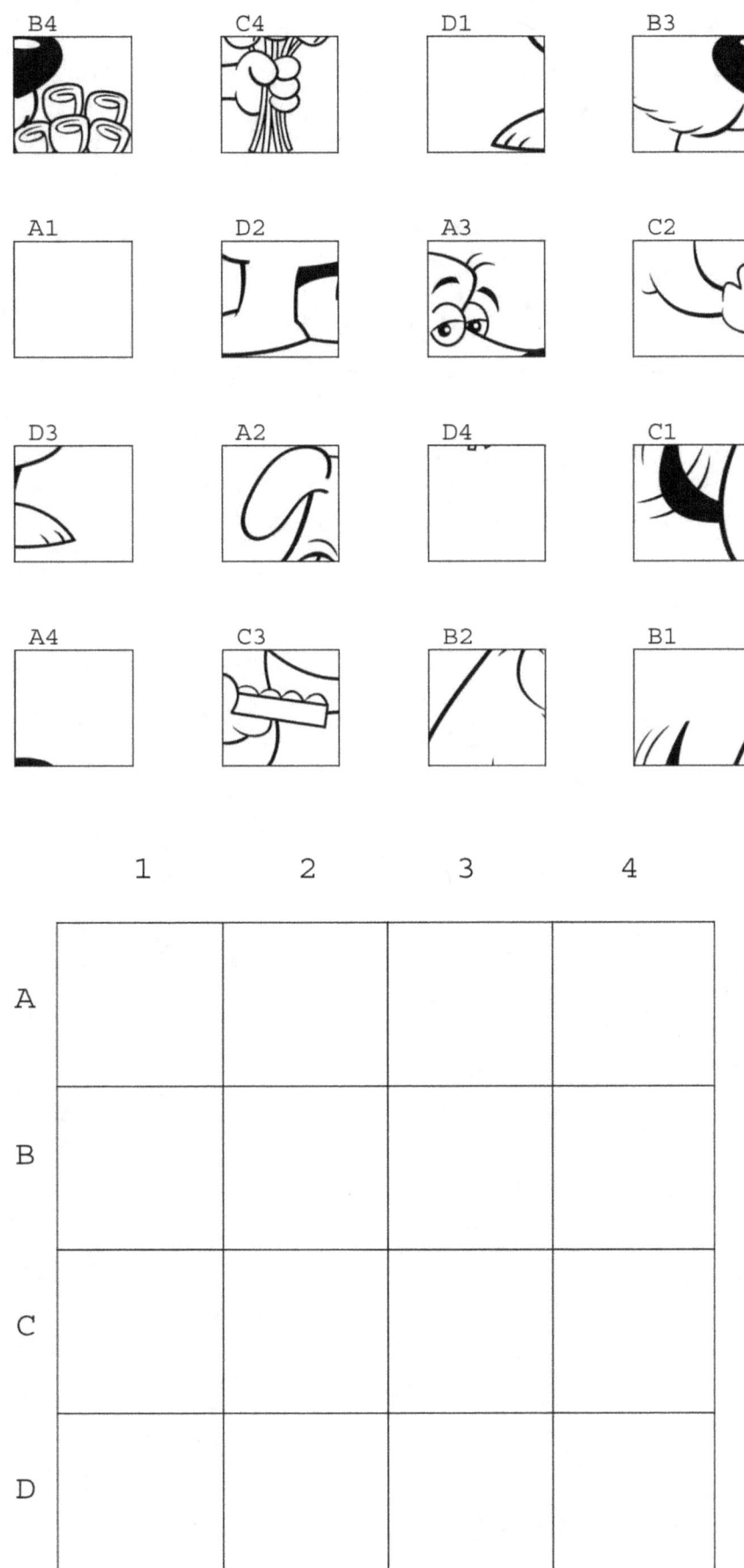

Thank you for completing our book! We appreciate your time and hope you enjoyed the experience. If you're up for more creative challenges, check out our other Pik-Jig books. Explore new grids and dive into the joy of artistic discovery. Happy drawing!

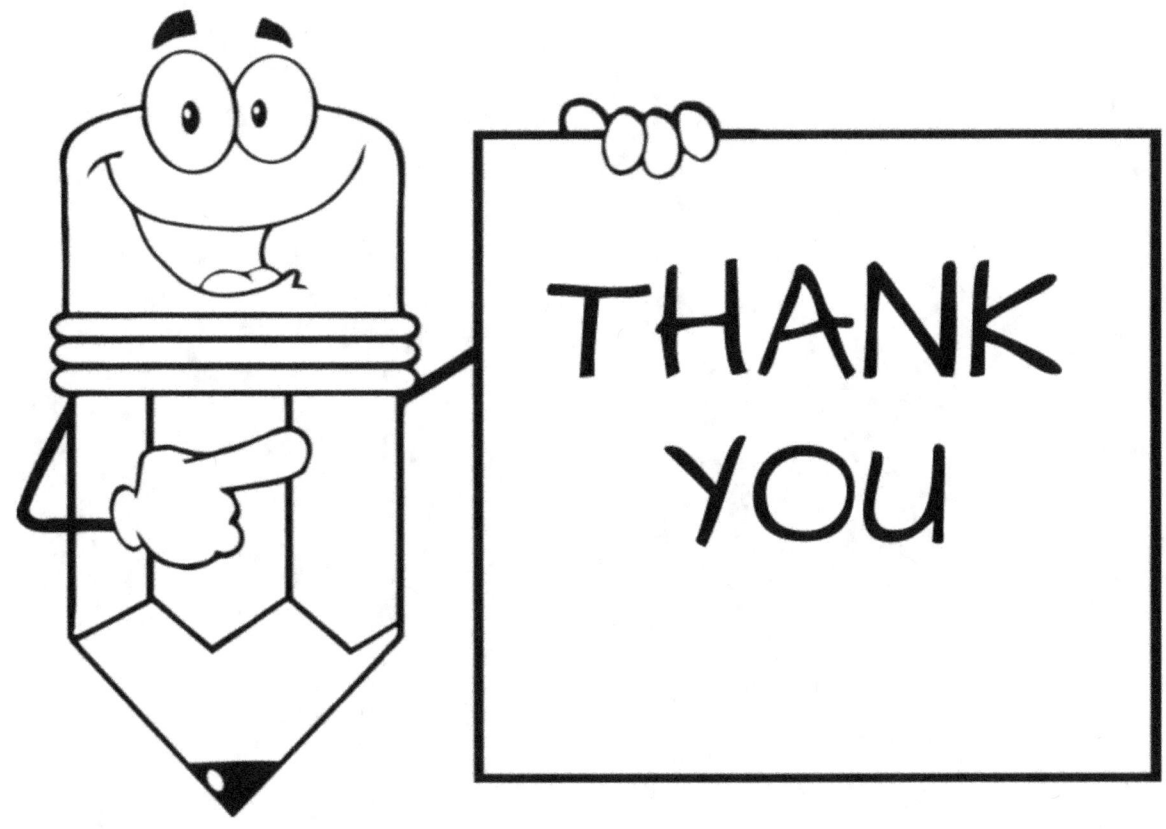

THANK YOU